Sustainable Fashion

by Paula N. Mugabi

A Wiley Brand

Sustainable Fashion For Dummies®

Published by: **John Wiley & Sons, Inc.**, 111 River Street, Hoboken, NJ 07030-5774, www.wiley.com

Copyright © 2023 by John Wiley & Sons, Inc., Hoboken, New Jersey

Media and software compilation copyright © 2023 by John Wiley & Sons, Inc. All rights reserved.

Published simultaneously in Canada

No part of this publication may be reproduced, stored in a retrieval system or transmitted in any form or by any means, electronic, mechanical, photocopying, recording, scanning or otherwise, except as permitted under Sections 107 or 108 of the 1976 United States Copyright Act, without the prior written permission of the Publisher. Requests to the Publisher for permission should be addressed to the Permissions Department, John Wiley & Sons, Inc., 111 River Street, Hoboken, NJ 07030, (201) 748-6011, fax (201) 748-6008, or online at http://www.wiley.com/go/permissions.

Trademarks: Wiley, For Dummies, the Dummies Man logo, Dummies.com, Making Everything Easier, and related trade dress are trademarks or registered trademarks of John Wiley & Sons, Inc. and may not be used without written permission. All other trademarks are the property of their respective owners. John Wiley & Sons, Inc. is not associated with any product or vendor mentioned in this book.

LIMIT OF LIABILITY/DISCLAIMER OF WARRANTY: WHILE THE PUBLISHER AND AUTHORS HAVE USED THEIR BEST EFFORTS IN PREPARING THIS WORK, THEY MAKE NO REPRESENTATIONS OR WARRANTIES WITH RESPECT TO THE ACCURACY OR COMPLETENESS OF THE CONTENTS OF THIS WORK AND SPECIFICALLY DISCLAIM ALL WARRANTIES, INCLUDING WITHOUT LIMITATION ANY IMPLIED WARRANTIES OF MERCHANTABILITY OR FITNESS FOR A PARTICULAR PURPOSE. NO WARRANTY MAY BE CREATED OR EXTENDED BY SALES REPRESENTATIVES, WRITTEN SALES MATERIALS OR PROMOTIONAL STATEMENTS FOR THIS WORK. THE FACT THAT AN ORGANIZATION, WEBSITE, OR PRODUCT IS REFERRED TO IN THIS WORK AS A CITATION AND/OR POTENTIAL SOURCE OF FURTHER INFORMATION DOES NOT MEAN THAT THE PUBLISHER AND AUTHORS ENDORSE THE INFORMATION OR SERVICES THE ORGANIZATION, WEBSITE, OR PRODUCT MAY PROVIDE OR RECOMMENDATIONS IT MAY MAKE. THIS WORK IS SOLD WITH THE UNDERSTANDING THAT THE PUBLISHER IS NOT ENGAGED IN RENDERING PROFESSIONAL SERVICES. THE ADVICE AND STRATEGIES CONTAINED HEREIN MAY NOT BE SUITABLE FOR YOUR SITUATION. YOU SHOULD CONSULT WITH A SPECIALIST WHERE APPROPRIATE. FURTHER, READERS SHOULD BE AWARE THAT WEBSITES LISTED IN THIS WORK MAY HAVE CHANGED OR DISAPPEARED BETWEEN WHEN THIS WORK WAS WRITTEN AND WHEN IT IS READ. NEITHER THE PUBLISHER NOR AUTHORS SHALL BE LIABLE FOR ANY LOSS OF PROFIT OR ANY OTHER COMMERCIAL DAMAGES, INCLUDING BUT NOT LIMITED TO SPECIAL, INCIDENTAL, CONSEQUENTIAL, OR OTHER DAMAGES.

For general information on our other products and services, please contact our Customer Care Department within the U.S. at 877-762-2974, outside the U.S. at 317-572-3993, or fax 317-572-4002. For technical support, please visit https://hub.wiley.com/community/support/dummies.

Wiley publishes in a variety of print and electronic formats and by print-on-demand. Some material included with standard print versions of this book may not be included in e-books or in print-on-demand. If this book refers to media such as a CD or DVD that is not included in the version you purchased, you may download this material at http://booksupport.wiley.com. For more information about Wiley products, visit www.wiley.com.

Library of Congress Control Number: 2023933137

ISBN 978-1-119-98622-5 (pbk); ISBN 978-1-119-98624-9 (ebk); ISBN 978-1-119-98623-2 (ebk)

SKY10044477_031523

Table of Contents

Introduction

Fashion is a wonderful and creative form of self-expression. It makes us look and feel good and can often become a part of our identity! Unfortunately, the fashion industry (the way we currently consume and manufacture clothing) contributes in many adverse ways to the climate crisis. Landfills are filling up with clothes that will not decompose for a generation! Factories used by the fashion industry are some of the worst polluters. Moreover, unsafe working conditions for garment workers and poverty wages are still the norm rather than the exception in the fashion industry. Many of us don't want our enjoyment of something so vital — our self-expression and inner fashionista — to endanger our planet or workers in the industry. And that's where sustainable fashion enters the runway!

This book guides you on a more sustainable way to approach fashion. It covers all aspects of sustainable fashion, from the fundamentals to tips on finding the best thrift finds and maximizing your wardrobe potential.

About This Book

This book has been structured as a complete A–Z guide on sustainable fashion, covering both the fundamentals and many discrete but important topics, such as how to find gems at a thrift store, washer and dryer settings to prolong the life of your clothes, and many more practical tips that can help you become a more sustainable fashion consumer.

The book is designed both for those who are just beginning to look into sustainable fashion and for seasoned sustainable fashion consumers. This book is practical, relatable, and accessible. It is as plain-spoken as they come; it's not at all pretentious and doesn't have a judgmental tone. And its small size makes it perfect for an adventure to the thrift store.

With this book, I aim to empower you to take the first steps to a more sustainable lifestyle (in great shoes, of course).

Foolish Assumptions

Dear reader, I made a few assumptions about you. No, you're no dummy; however, you're reading this book because you want to build up your knowledge of sustainable fashion and, hopefully, consume fashion more sustainably. Here are some things I assumed about you and why you picked up this book:

» You want to gain more knowledge about sustainable fashion in general and what goes into making fashion sustainable.

» You want to gradually wean off fast fashion (trendy inexpensive mass-produced fashion), in favor of sustainable and ethical fashion.

» You understand that building sustainable fashion habits takes time and will be patient with yourself.

» You understand that incorporating sustainable fashion habits is a work in progress and that perhaps there isn't such a thing as being a perfect sustainable fashion consumer — but you're willing to do as much as you practically can.

Icons Used in This Book

Throughout this book, icons in the margins highlight certain types of valuable information called out for your attention. Here are the icons you'll encounter and a brief description of each.

TIP

The Tip icon provides shortcuts to help you more easily achieve the sustainable fashion outcomes I discuss in this book.

REMEMBER

Remember icons highlight really important information in the chapter — information that you should take away from the chapter if nothing else. If you are skimming through the chapter, take note of this icon and read the text next to it.

TECHNICAL STUFF

The Technical Stuff icon marks additional information of a more technical nature that you can skip over if you choose.

WARNING

The Warning icon tells you to watch out! It highlights important information on what you should avoid or information on actions with undesirable sustainability impacts.

Beyond the Book

In addition to what you're reading right now, this book comes with a free access-anywhere Cheat Sheet that includes tips to help you get started on your sustainable fashion journey and understand all that sustainable fashion lingo. To get this Cheat Sheet, simply go to www.dummies.com and type **Sustainable Fashion For Dummies Cheat Sheet** in the Search box.

Where to Go from Here

Unlike your favorite novel, you don't need to start with Chapter 1. In fact, you don't need to read this book in order at all! Key terms are defined in each chapter, so you won't get lost even if you skip chapters. The book has five parts, and each part is broken into chapters; you may read by part, by chapter, or even flip back and forth between chapters in any random order.

If you are new to sustainability and sustainable fashion, I recommend beginning with Chapter 1 to take a look at some fundamental concepts and get an overview of individual topics covered in the book. But if you sort of know your way around sustainability already and want a deeper dive on a specific topic, take your pick from the table of contents. For example, if you really want to find out more about taking care of your clothes, Part 4, on keeping your clothes and shoes in tip-top condition, has three chapters on this topic. If you want to know more about recycling your old clothes, check out Chapter 9. If you are ready to shop for new, sustainable clothes but don't know which brands to trust, take a peek at the list of sustainable brands in Chapter 13.

REMEMBER

Wherever you go, keep in mind that every small change you read about in this book and incorporate in your life makes an impact. Thanks for going on this journey with me!

1

Opening the Door to Sustainable Fashion

IN THIS PART . . .

Grasp the basics of sustainability and sustainable fashion.

Start your sustainable fashion journey by maximizing the potential of the clothes you already have in your closet.

Understand the true costs of fast fashion and find out how to identify and avoid it.

Develop more sustainable fashion consumption habits.

IN THIS CHAPTER

» Seeing what sustainability means for people and the planet

» Recognizing unsustainable practices in the fashion industry

» Looking at your role in the fashion industry's transition to sustainability

» Getting started on your sustainable fashion journey

Chapter **1**

Closet, Meet Sustainable Fashion

You've decided to start your sustainable fashion journey (or maybe just give it a try), but as with anything new, you're a bit overwhelmed. I get it. There's an overload of information out there! Sifting through it all and finding a way to feel like you're making a difference can be stressful. You've probably seen pictures of landfills filled with clothes and read startling statistics about the environmental damage from the fashion industry, but you tell yourself that you don't make or sell clothes, so how can you make a difference? I'm here to help you figure things out.

In this chapter, I help you get started with the basics. I help you understand what sustainability truly means, how the fashion industry is contributing to the climate crisis, how some stakeholders in the fashion industry are trying to do things better, how you can become a sustainable fashion consumer. Most importantly, I show you how to be part of the solution while avoiding *eco-anxiety* (the fear of environmental disaster that comes from observing the impact of climate change).

Understanding Sustainability

The dictionary defines sustainable or sustainability as the avoidance of (or reduction of) the depletion of natural resources to maintain ecological balance. The terms sustainable or sustainability, in general, tend to describe how humans must change how they consume natural resources to slow climate change and ultimately reverse it. But simply put, it is living our everyday lives, doing all the things we do in a way that is not harmful to our planet so that we live in harmony with nature.

This section covers some foundational concepts around sustainability.

Preserving our planet and preventing climate change

The conventional definition or understanding of sustainability tends to focus on eco-friendliness, particularly on pollution and climate change.

A person or population's impact on the environment is measured and referred to as a *carbon footprint* (which is the total amount of greenhouse gases — including carbon dioxide and methane — that are generated by all our actions. The average carbon footprint for a person in the United States is 16 tons per year, one of the highest rates in the world. There are many ways to reduce your carbon footprint, like by eating less meat or using public transport, but those methods are beyond the scope of this book. In this book, I help you reduce your carbon footprint by shopping sustainably, purchasing less clothing, and sending your unwanted clothing or textiles to other places besides a landfill.

Treating people with dignity and respect

The environmental aspects of sustainability are critical, but there is another important aspect of sustainability: ethical practices.

Fashion is sustainable if the clothes and accessories are made in an eco-friendly, ethical, and socially responsible way. The socially responsible aspect of sustainability in fashion means that clothes and shoes are made in a way that is fair to workers and the farmers who grow the crops for fabric, such as cotton. Workers should work in safe environments and receive adequate wages.

The ethical aspect of sustainability in fashion means that there is a fair and transparent supply chain, with fashion brands directing their business to factories that are audited and accredited for fair labor practices or sourcing fabric from fair-trade farms. I discuss this in more detail in Chapter 5.

For me, sustainable fashion must incorporate the ethical aspect I describe earlier, but you will see that many commentators or authors sometimes use the terms "ethical fashion" and "sustainable fashion" interchangeably, and other times as if the terms refer to entirely different things. To me, the ethical aspect is a part of sustainability.

Calling Out the Problem with Today's Fashion Industry

The fashion industry has an overproduction problem, and this overproduction is part of what makes the fashion industry the least sustainable, one of the worst polluting industries, and the one with the most unethical practices. New stuff comes into stores every week, our closets are bulging with clothes, and charity stores are receiving record amounts of clothing donations because there are just too many clothes entering circulation. It is estimated that 100 billion clothes are produced annually. That's the equivalent of 12 new pieces of clothing per year per person, and whether these clothes are bought or not, they are still made. Those statistics explain why we have clothes piling up in landfills. We are consuming 60 percent more clothes now than we did 20 years ago and throwing away a lot of them. Also, a lot of the waste comes from fashion factories in the form of excess fabric that isn't used in garment production and is thrown away.

The rise of fast fashion

So what has happened in the last 20 years? Why do we all own more clothes? The 60 percent increase correlates with the rise of fast fashion. *Fast fashion* is an approach to the design, creation, and marketing of clothing fashions that emphasizes making fashion trends quickly and cheaply available to consumers. Fast fashion equates to quick production, high volume, trendy items, and inexpensive prices at the register. (But that doesn't necessarily mean the clothes cost less! Chapter 6 explains the concept of cost per wear.)

Fast fashion appeared in the 1990s and early 2000s and has taken the industry by storm, providing more variety and a greater volume of clothes than we have probably ever seen — or needed.

REMEMBER

Fast fashion is the norm right now, but there was a vibrant fashion world before fast fashion. Many well-known brands predate fast fashion, and they were viable, successful businesses back then.

A three-legged monster

The fast-fashion model relies on churning out lots and lots of trendy clothes very quickly, which in turn is heavily dependent on fast, on-demand manufacturing and uses a lot of resources. The end product — literally tons of clothes — ends up in landfills as soon as a trend is out of style. Consequently, the problem with fast fashion is threefold:

>> **The fashion industry has become an environmental disaster.** According to the World Economic Forum, fashion production makes up 10 percent of humanity's carbon emissions. Dyeing and constructing clothes leads to water pollution, and the final product ends up polluting the land when it's tossed into a landfill. But that's not all. Today, most clothes are made with synthetic (man-made) materials that take decades to decompose, emitting greenhouse gases in the process. These gases trap heat in our atmosphere and contribute to climate change.

>> **Garments workers are treated poorly.** This breakneck speed of production means that clothes need to be in and out of the factory in two to three weeks and workers must work arduous hours, often in unsafe conditions. On top of all that, most of the time, garment workers aren't even paid a *living wage* (an income that keeps a worker out of poverty).

>> **The modern mass-market fashion industry's business model scams you, the consumer.** What seems like a good deal when you have options galore weekly at apparently

cheap prices is not a good deal. That's because if you aren't spending a lot of money on an item, chances are, it's made with poor-quality materials. Once it falls apart, you need to buy a new one. And then another one. In the end, you probably would've been better off buying a higher-quality, but more expensive, item at the start. This concept is a key component of cost per wear, which I explain in Chapter 6.

REMEMBER

Most fashion brands try to convince consumers to buy more than they need. That works for them, because you give them more money, but it's not good for your wallet or the environment.

Being Part of the Solution and Avoiding Eco-Anxiety

The scale of the problematic practices of the fashion industry may make it seem as if individual action can't have any meaningful impact in reversing the adverse impacts of such practices. The more you read or hear about the problem, the more you are at risk for *eco-anxiety*, a chronic fear of environmental doom and feeling helpless about it

Even if that's not you, you may still wonder where you fit in all of this. You don't make clothes; you just buy them. You still need clothes and still want to enjoy fashion, but you don't want it to be at the expense of the planet and the people who make your clothes. You also know that precious resources go into making your clothes. Armed with this information, you can and should make more sustainable fashion choices. This book explains what those choices are and helps you implement them.

You may be one person, but your choices and actions have an impact! The actions of each one of us ultimately add up to become a catalyst for good, meaningful change in the fashion industry. So don't aim to change the world by yourself; you'll get frustrated and quit, and the planet can't afford you quitting.

The fact is that fashion's adverse impacts are primarily caused by the fast-fashion brands that produce all the clothes. If it weren't for their manufacturing of hauls of these clothes, fashion consumption wouldn't have changed in the ways it has. The industry is the cause of the problem and the primary culprit, of course; but by consuming fast fashion the way the industry wants you to, you become a sort of accomplice after the fact.

So, what actions can you take as an individual? I believe wholeheartedly that if many more people were to bring sustainable values to the consumption of fashion, brands might be forced to do better. It may sound whimsical, but there are definitely more and more fashion consumers who value sustainability, so a domino effect can't be discounted.

Show fashion brands that you don't support their unsustainable practices by boycotting their products. As brands plan for the future, the wiser ones will listen and make changes. While your individual actions may seem like they're too small to have any impact, aggregated with similar actions of others, the impact becomes meaningful. Plus, there is an emotional benefit to you. It feels good to know that you're doing your part by, among other things, shopping more intentionally and mindfully. Once you begin living your values as a sustainable fashion consumer, you can be an inspiration to others in your orbit.

TIP

You can also work on educating yourself about the issues from reliable sources. You can follow environmental bloggers or sustainable fashion bloggers and read ethical fashion publications like *Good On You*. With more information, you can become involved in more targeted engagement, including petitioning brands to make the changes necessary to operate more sustainably.

Taking Action: What You Can Do to Increase Sustainability

Here I provide you with information on some specific actions you can take. There are many ways to be a sustainable, ethical fashion consumer. There is always something, however small, you can do to make your fashion consumption more sustainable. All these actions are discussed in more detail in various chapters of this book. Each action references the chapter where it is discussed in more detail so you can skip ahead to the individual chapters as you like.

REMEMBER

Sustainable fashion habits are built over time. Don't aim to do everything at once. For example, it may take you some time to learn how to sew to repair your clothes, but you can shop for preloved items or from your own closet right away. Also, perfect sustainability doesn't exist; don't let seeking perfection be the enemy of your progress.

Try these tips to get started on the road to sustainability:

>> **Use what you already own.** Your most sustainable clothes are the ones you already own, including your fast-fashion clothes. Resources have already gone into making these clothes so take care of them! That'll help them last longer, keeping them in your closet and out of landfills. Chapter 10 walks you through some best practices for clothing care. For help styling your clothes, check out Chapter 2.

>> **Repair the clothes in your closet.** A great way to be a sustainable fashion consumer is to repair your clothes. This keeps your clothes in your closet and out of landfills. The task may seem daunting, but you can make some simple repairs without a sewing machine. For the bigger repairs, you can take clothes to a tailor. Chapter 11 guides you through some basic sewing techniques, repair methods, and *upcycling* (making something new out of your old clothes).

>> **Buy preloved clothes.** This not only keeps clothes out of landfills and prevents the resulting environmental damage, but also gets you great stuff for less. Ready to get thrifting? Check out Chapters 7 and 8.

>> **Shop from sustainable brands.** Chapter 5 helps you figure out what to look for in a clothing brand, and Chapter 13 includes a list of brands I love.

>> **Donate and recycle what you no longer need.** At some point you might fall out love of with clothes and need to give them away or recycle them. In Chapter 9, I guide you through this process so you can get rid of your textiles sustainably.

Chapter **2**

Starting with the Clothes You Already Own

I n the sustainable social media world, you may come across this advice: Shop your closet. Your closet is the best and easiest place to set off on your sustainable fashion journey! The most sustainable fashion is the clothes you already own. Phew! You don't have to spend any money to get started on your sustainable fashion journey!

Sustainable fashion is typically defined as fashion that is produced in an eco-friendly and socially responsible manner. Efforts are made to minimize the impact on the earth, and clothes are made in factories where garment workers are paid fairly and work in a safe and hospitable environment. (For more on what makes a fashion brand sustainable, turn to Chapter 5.)

But as a fashion consumer, your understanding of sustainable fashion should include how you can make sustainable fashion *choices*. This means consuming fashion more mindfully, buying only the clothes you need, and wearing the clothes you have (and not throwing them away prematurely).

In this chapter, I help you maximize your closet by loving the clothes you have, exploring their potential, and embracing your personal style.

Taking Stock of Your Closet

You can find yourself shopping unnecessarily because you have no clue what is hiding in a messy closet (no judgment — this happens to all of us!) or because you haven't taken the time to explore what type of clothes work (and don't work) for you or haven't figured out your personal style. To avoid unnecessary shopping, audit and organize your closet so you know what you have. The prospect of doing this may have you running for the hills, but it's one of those things that you need to do to get your sustainable journey off on the right foot.

Auditing your closet

Auditing your closet allows you to know what you have. Closets are places where you keep stuff, but they can also be places where you lose track of your stuff. Auditing your closet once or twice a year helps you to refocus on what you have, what has or hasn't worked for you, and what you forgot you had. By doing this you better position yourself to make more mindful fashion purchases.

REMEMBER

A closet audit in the context of sustainable fashion consumption is not a purge or decluttering exercise but rather an exercise to discover your style and to enable you to make more sustainable fashion choices in the future. You may still need to purge, but that's not the goal. You can clear your closet, perhaps with professional help, but it will be filled up again in no time if you do it simply as part of a purge exercise. A professional wardrobe organizer once told me that she helped someone clear out closets only to come back and find the closets full again. You should use the audit to really understand what kind of clothes work for you.

Auditing your closet is a way to discover your personal style. Knowing your personal style is helpful as you work on becoming a sustainable fashion consumer. You'll be able to stay away from trend-chasing and avoid buying stuff you don't actually like merely because it's on sale. You won't suffer finding new clothes with the tags still attached years after they were bought — clothes that you're likely to throw away because they don't fit your style. Auditing your closet contributes directly to fewer clothes in land-fills, and it also saves you money.

To get started, take all your clothes out of the closet and dump them in a pile on your bed. If this sounds overwhelming and messy, don't worry; you'll love your closet much more after you've gone through the process.

As British novelist John Galsworthy commented, "Beginnings are always messy," but you've got this.

TIP

The following steps guide you through the process and, hopefully, make it less daunting.

1. **Set aside time on a day that you are not too busy.**

   You'll need a few hours, maybe three or four.

2. **Get a notebook or use the notes app on your smartphone to take notes.**

   You can use them to document your style discoveries and findings during the process.

3. **Set a relaxing atmosphere.**

   For example, put on some good music or stream a favorite TV show in the background.

4. **Take all your clothes out of your closet and put them in a pile on your bed.**

5. **Sort your clothes into three piles: Nos; Yeses; and Maybes:**

   - **The No pile:** Think about why you don't like or wear these clothes, especially if they are still in good condition; you want to understand why they didn't work for you. It may be the cut of the pants (maybe you favor low-rise over high-rise pants, for example) or perhaps you don't like the quality of a specific brand of clothes. Whatever the reason, take notes or make a mental note not to buy these types of clothes again. These are clothes you are probably going to get rid of. But don't throw your "no-go" clothes in the trash! Chapter 9 tells you how to donate and dispose of clothes responsibly.

   - **The Yes pile:** The clothes in this pile give you an indication of your personal style. These clothes are probably the ones you wear the most. Note your specific preferences: for example, the length of the skirts, the cut of the pants, the colors of the clothes, and so on.

WARNING

- You may be tempted to put some pieces in the yes pile that don't really belong there. These are pieces that you have some kind of emotional attachment to. Maybe they were expensive, or you hope to wear them in the future. A good practice is to try on your Yes clothes. See how you feel in them and consider where you'll wear them, when you last wore them, and whether they fit with your lifestyle.

- **The Maybe pile:** These are clothes that may have potential. Try styling them or, if they're in season, try wearing them that week to see how you feel about them.

Phew! Now that you are done auditing your closet, you can begin to sort the mess. Put the clothes in the Yes and Maybe piles back in your closet. (The section titled "Organizing your closet" helps you do that properly.) The clothes in the No pile should be donated, given to friends and family, or sold (more on this in Chapter 9). Put them in a box or container. Work on getting them a new home as soon as you can.

WARNING

You may be reading this book to explore ways to avoid *fast fashion* (mass-produced, trends-focused, and inexpensive fashion). For more on fast fashion, read Chapter 3. Even if you are super eager to shut the door on fast fashion, you shouldn't rush to throw away the items you own. Doing so would be wasteful, which is the opposite of sustainable!

REMEMBER

The clothes you may have fallen out of love with in your "no" or "maybe" piles may just need some alteration for a new look or better fit.

Sometimes we fall out of love with clothes because of fit issues. Ready-to-wear clothes are made for "average" body shapes, but the definition of average is limited, and most of us may have do some adjustments. Fit issues can always be addressed by alterations. An alteration that resizes a piece of clothing you haven't worn in a while may bring back the love. Chapter 11 includes more info about how tailors can help you feel and look better in your clothes.

EMBRACING PERSONAL STYLE IN AN ERA OF TRENDS AND FAST FASHION

Embracing your personal style and sustainable fashion are closely linked. In a fast-fashion, trend-focused world, you can lose your personal style to trends. It happens because of the heavy marketing and the success of fast-fashion influencers and celebrities. You can find yourself spending money on trendy clothes that are designed to last only until the next trends come out, leading to a throwaway culture and excessive consumerism. And even with a lot of clothes, you may still be frustrated, think you have nothing to wear, or feel like you just aren't happy with your clothes. Ultimately, fashion should work for you and not the other way around.

An article from *Harper's Bazaar UK*, titled "As we move away from trends, there's never been a better time to find your personal style," suggests that trends and copycat fashion are dying out in favor of personal style and how this is a sustainable approach to fashion.

As a sustainable consumer, you want your closet to have mindfully created pieces, pieces that you love and see yourself having for a long time. Be an individual, reject the notion that you have to be on-trend, and take the time to discover your personal style.

TIP

Have a system in place to recognize clothes you aren't wearing. This will make auditing less stressful next time. A good one is the reverse hanger method. Reverse your hangers to face out instead of in, and when you wear a piece, turn the hanger to face in. This can help you keep track of what you are wearing these days.

Organizing your closet

An organized closet means that when you open it you are inspired to wear the clothes you have — not overwhelmed by the mess that hides your clothes and sends you rushing to the store to buy more. I have bought the same hoodie twice because I forgot that I had the exact same one, which was tucked away in a place where I didn't think to check for it.

There is no one standard way to organize a closet, but the goal should be to make your clothes easily identifiable, tidy, and visually inspiring. Here are some ways to create that ideal closet setup:

TIP

>> **Organize by color.** If you have a colorful closet, organizing by color is a logical way to easily identify your clothes.

>> **Organize by category.** Keep clothes of the same category in one place. If you have a colorful closet, organize it by color and then by category: for example, yellow dresses, yellow pants, then green dresses, green pants, and so forth.

>> **Organize and rotate by season.** Have the clothes you need for the current season most accessible. I live in New York City and have limited closet space, so I have to store some off-season items and swap them out when seasons change. You can also put off-season items on higher shelves and put in-season items on more accessible shelves.

>> **Create space for movement.** Your closet shouldn't be so jam-packed that you can't easily get to or see your clothes. Consider getting smaller hangers that take up less space or potentially putting away some clothes to free up space.

>> **File-fold your foldable clothes.** File-fold so you can easily see and sort through your clothes. Don't stack your T-shirts on top of each other such that when you pull one out, they all tend to fall over. Stacking also makes it harder to reach clothes at bottom of the stack. Instead, fold your clothes into small rectangles and store them vertically in your drawer, like files in a filing cabinet. This way, you can see all the pieces in your drawer at once.

>> **Keep your closet visually appealing.** Use matching hangers, fold your clothes neatly, and clean your closet often.

REMEMBER

Advertisements may try to encourage you to buy a closet organization system. But buying more things is part of that unsustainable consumerism you want to avoid. You don't need any complicated storage systems for your closet to look fresh and inspiring.

Unlocking the Wow Factor in Clothes You Already Own

Your clothes may have more styling potential than you think. Have fun styling your clothes and coming up with ways to wear them differently. You may be uninspired by (or maybe just ignoring) some clothes in your closet because you don't know what to do with them. Maybe they looked great on the mannequin or model, but you don't know how to make them work for you. Before passing these clothes on to someone else, give them another shot. You may just need a few styling tips. When you know how to style your clothes, you are less likely to throw them away prematurely or always be shopping because you think you have nothing to wear.

In this section, I hope to renew an excitement for the clothes you already own, which is an easy and inexpensive way to start your sustainable journey. I suggest a few ideas for you to draw inspiration from. You don't have to use them all, but you can probably pick up some tips from each section. You'll come to appreciate how to match your colors, prints, and accessories.

TIP

The path toward a sustainable lifestyle and away from excessive consumerism requires gratitude. Aesop said, "Gratitude turns what we have into enough," and that quote inspired me to make necessary changes to my wardrobe and shopping habits. I hope it helps you too.

Knowing the color wheel

A *color wheel* is a circle diagram that illustrates the relationship between colors. Most simple color wheels have at least six colors that include primary colors (red, yellow, and blue) and secondary colors (orange, green, and purple); more extensive ones include tertiary colors. Tertiary colors are those that come from mixing one of the primary colors with one of the nearest secondary colors: Red + Orange = Red-orange, Yellow + Orange = Yellow-orange, Blue + Purple = Blue-purple and so on.

TECHNICAL
STUFF

Color wheels aren't new. The first color wheel was invented by Isaac Newton, as documented in his work called *Opticks*. The invention clearly involved deep science, but hey, it is also an amazing style tool! It has since evolved and been improved upon by others.

Knowing what colors go together give you a lot of potential for creating outfits. Using a color wheel exposes you to lots of possible color combinations. Search for an image of a color wheel online so you can get started.

Don't be too hesitant to try these combinations. They work because they are based on proven science, so just trust the process!

Here are the basic takeaways:

>> **Analogous colors match well.** Colors that are next to each other on the color wheel go well together. For example, greens and blues match, oranges and yellows match, and so on. The same logic applies to different shades of the same color.

>> **Complementary colors match well.** Colors that are on opposite sides of the color wheel (across from each other) go well together. Now you can see why green and red go well together, as well as purple and yellow, orange and blue, and lots of other combinations.

TIP

If you have a colorful closet, you may want to organize it by the color wheel. It can inspire you to try different color combinations.

TECHNICAL
STUFF

If you've looked at the color wheel, you're probably wondering how black, white, and gray fit into the color scheme. Black, white, and gray (gray is a mix of white and black) are not technically colors because they don't have specific wavelengths, which are what define colors. These "colors" — or should I say "non-colors" — match with nearly all other colors.

Mixing prints and patterns

You may have some prints in your closet that you don't know how to style. Looking for some suggestions? Here are some ways to wear your prints and patterns:

>> **Wear prints and patterns under something more neutral for a more understated look.** You may have bought some prints on a whim and don't feel like you can match them with any of your clothes. Consider styling them under something more neutral, such as a blazer, which will cover the print and reveal only a little of it.

>> **Mix different prints for a fun, bold look.** Conventional wisdom says that you can't mix prints, but that's old news. You *can* mix prints. I am very active on the social media fashion scene, and I have seen people come up with the most stylish outfits. You just need to get more comfortable exploring the clothes you have.

You can mix prints or patterns of the same tonal range or color: for example, dark polka dots with a dark floral print. You can also pair a smaller print with a bigger print: for example, a bold stripe with a simple stripe.

There are many ways to mix prints that can't all be covered here, but there are numerous places you can go to get inspiration. Pinterest is a good place to start. Just search using the words "mixed prints." You can also look to brands that are well known for mixed prints, like Farm Rio, Free People, DVF (Diane von Furstenberg), and so on. You might be able to create similar looks from your closet!

REMEMBER

Style is a form of personal expression. While prints and patterns are not for everyone, they may be for you! Trends shouldn't dictate what you like, so don't throw out prints and patterns you like just because they may not be on-trend currently.

Accessorizing for a different look

It may sound cliché to say that accessories make a look, but they do. Accessories have the power to elevate an outfit from "fine" to "fabulous."

Before you rush to buy new clothes because you're bored with the clothes you have, reach into your accessories drawer! Accessories can help you give an outfit a new look, allowing you to make do with fewer clothes but still look stylish. You can literally transform a white T-shirt and blue jeans from soccer mom to brunch-ready to business lunch by changing accessories. This transformation of outfits with accessories has become kind of a specialty of mine.

TIP

Keep your accessories organized so you can easily see them for inspiration. Hang your hats on hooks in one place and keep a neat jewelry box or a jewelry tree. Organize your shoes by season and type so you know where all your heels are, for example, and can easily try them on as you plan outfits.

Invest time in building a collection of useful accessories that you can change up for multiple outfits. Belts, hats, sunglasses, scarves, and earrings are examples of accessories you should have. Layering pieces like jackets and coats are accessories too! Remember jackets and coats are great items to thrift. (See Chapter 15 for a list of great items to thrift.) And don't forget shoes. Make sure you have the right shoes for different occasions, so you can easily change up your outfits. (Chapter 17 provides a list of great sustainable shoe brands.)

Using styling apps

If you find style tips overwhelming, you should know that there are lots of apps that can help simplify styling the clothes in your closet for you. If you watched *Clueless* in the 1990s like me, you were probably blown away by Cher's computerized closet. Now there are apps that can help you plan outfits just like Cher did — but in a much more modern way. They essentially digitize your wardrobe so that you can see the clothes in your closet on your phone. With the versatile new technologies available today, Cher from *Clueless* can well and truly move over!

Apps are available on iOS and Android, including Smart Closet, My Wardrobe, Cladwell, Pureple, Stylebook, and more to help you plan outfits.

TIP

Look up reviews online before committing to an app and uploading your photos. YouTube has a lot of content with reviews, walkthroughs of the apps, and app comparisons.

They all work slightly differently, but all have the same goal: to help you style clothes in your closet and buy only what you need to complete your wardrobe. Typically, you need to upload photos of your clothes. The app then generates some outfit suggestions for you. You can also style yourself by dragging and dropping photos of your clothes and then creating outfits. On some of the apps, like Stylebook, you can upload photos from Pinterest to re-create outfits from your own clothes. The apps also facilitate vacation outfit planning.

TIP

When you discover a great outfit combination, take a picture so you remember it. You can create an album on your phone. Also, some of the outfit planners have a feature that allows you to save your favorite looks!

These apps can also provide style intel, like which clothes you have worn the most and the least, and what colors you wear most. This can help you along your journey to figure out your personal style.

Some apps, such as Cladwell, have style inspiration templates. You can select and build outfits from what you have based on those templates, and the apps will make suggestions on how and where to shop for any items missing from an outfit, allowing you to shop mindfully. Others have style guides to help you find some inspiration.

TIP

Getting started requires you to take photos of your clothes, which may be a pain, especially if you have a lot of clothes. To simplify this process, upload seasonally and focus on the current season. Another good time to do it is after a closet audit; take photos of the clothes as you put them back in your closet.

Using apps to style your clothes is probably a new concept to you, and starting anything new can have some hiccups, but give it a go! Some of the outfit suggestions may seem a little different from what you're familiar with, but they might actually work.

Working with Outfit Formulas

Another way you can simplify styling is to use *outfit formulas,* which are style templates to help you create different outfits from clothes you already have. Stylists over the years have figured out some formulas for outfit success. Outfit formulas help reduce decision fatigue and take the overwhelm out of putting outfits together. Lots of outfit formulas are out there for varied personal styles, so it's not a one-size-fits-all situation. Chances are good you can find one that suits your personal style.

Defining outfit formulas

If the term "outfit formula" sounds methodological, that's because it is! These formulas are tried and tested to create outfit combinations that work well to build stylish outfits. Here's an example:

> blazer + white T-shirt+ medium or dark wash (not ripped) jeans + heels/flats = a dressy denim look

This combination looks great on most people.

Outfit formulas not only save you time getting dressed in the morning but also offer some tangible benefits from a sustainability perspective. They are an additional tool you can use to help you make the most of your clothes. They reduce decision fatigue, which often sends you rushing out the door to shop because you feel like you have nothing to wear. Outfit formulas are cheat sheets for great styling.

REMEMBER

If you feel good in your clothes, you're less likely to throw them away.

Plugging in outfit formulas

So many outfit formulas are available that I can't attempt to cover them all here. But for those of you who are new to the concept of outfit formulas, Table 2-1 starts you off with some formulas for common pieces you probably already have in your closet. Some of the formulas have color suggestions, but don't limit yourself to the suggested colors. Use a color wheel to discover different color combinations (refer to "Knowing the color wheel," earlier in this chapter).

Looking for some visual inspiration? See Figures 2-1 and 2-2 for two outfits I created using two outfit formulas from Table 2-1. The outfits are created from two wardrobe staples, black denim and black pants styled with pieces that most people have in their closets. The outfit combination in Figure 2-1 was one I hadn't tried before, and it was a hit for me. Who knew that a simple tee and black pants could be so fun and chic?

TABLE 2-1 **Simple Outfit Formulas to Get You Started**

Black Pants (Straight Leg)

Casual look: white tee (tucked in) + denim jacket + flats/classic sneakers

Dressy look: white blouse + black blazer + heels

Black Denim

Casual look: plaid shirt + sneakers/ankle boots

Dressy look: button down shirt + simple jewelry + heels

Dark-Wash Blue Denim

Casual look: floral top + long cardigan + flats

Dressy look: white tee + black blazer + heels

Light-Wash Blue Denim

Casual look: black tee/bodysuit + black leather jacket + flats/ankle boots/sneakers

Dressy look: black camisole/tee + black blazer + heels

Black Leggings

Casual look: black oversized jumper/sweatshirt /hoodie + trench coat/overcoat + sneakers

Dressy look: oversized-white button-down shirt + simple jewelry + strappy sandals/flats

Linen Shorts

Casual look: white blouse + sandals

Dressy look: tank top + linen blazer + strappy heels/ sandals

Floral Dress/Skirt

Casual look: light cardigan (in one of the colors on the dress or a neutral color) + white classic sneakers

Dressy look: white or black sweater (tucked or half tucked) + simple jewelry + leather jacket/blazer + boots

Photo credit: Mariama Hutson

FIGURE 2-1: Outfit formula for a casual look with black pants: White tee, denim jacket, and sneakers.

REMEMBER

These formulas are not intended to make you shop but to help you style what you already have. The outfits in Figures 2-1 and 2-2 were created from clothes I had in my closet.

There are lots of outfit formulas out there. You will find useful ideas on YouTube and Pinterest. I personally have gotten a lot of visual inspiration from there.

WARNING

Fashion content on social media is disproportionately geared toward fast-fashion shopping, which can lead to impulse buying. I advise that you use images from social media as inspiration for what you can do with what you already have in your closet, not for shopping.

Photo credit: Mariama Hutson

FIGURE 2-2: Outfit formula for a dressy look with black jeans: Black blouse, simple jewelry, and heels.

IN THIS CHAPTER

» **Understanding the negative impact of fast fashion**

» **Knowing fast fashion when you see it**

» **Making the move to sustainability**

» **Calling out greenwashing (fast fashion in disguise)**

Chapter **3**
Adios, Fast Fashion

When you think fast fashion, brands like Shein and Fashion Nova may come to mind. These brands are the epitome of fast fashion. *Fast fashion* in very simple terms is synonymous with fast, high-volume, trendy, and inexpensive fashion. Fast fashion emphasizes making fashion trends available to consumers quickly and cheaply.

What's considered fast fashion today is a recent fashion phenomenon, not even 40 years old. A *New York Times* article from 1989 titled "Two stores that cruise the fashion first lane" describes the early years of fast fashion. The article describes how by buying from Zara and Express, a young woman can change her clothes as often as she changes her lipstick. Flash forward 30 years: Fast fashion is the biggest player in the fashion industry, but its ascent to a dominant position has had devastating adverse impacts on the environment and garment workers. Fast fashion has altered the fashion industry landscape in numerous ways, including how much is produced, how much is consumed, and how much is wasted/thrown away, generally making fashion disposable.

This chapter defines the inverse of sustainable fashion: fast fashion. I give you the scoop on the negative social and environmental impact of fast fashion and help you recognize it in your closet and out in the world. I also advise you about the deceptive business of greenwashing. This chapter aims to foster more sustainable fashion choices and equip you with the tools to push fashion brands to change their practices and do better.

Identifying the Real Cost of Fast Fashion

Fast fashion continues its devastating toll on the environment, workers, our wallets, and even our happiness. In the last 30 years, the way we have consumed fashion has shifted drastically with mostly adverse consequences.

The following sections explain the economic, social, and environmental impacts that are the result of millions of garments being produced and consumed every year.

Looking at the fast-fashion business model

To understand the repercussions of fast fashion, it's important to understand the fast-fashion business model. A 2003 Harvard Business case study on Zara explains that Zara achieved spectacular growth via a design-on-demand business model, whereby Zara can design, make, and deliver garments in two weeks, allowing it to always have something fresh in its stores. The traditional fashion models design and manufacture for a season and typically have two seasons, spring/summer and fall/winter, but Zara is doing this every two weeks for consumers in multiple countries. When I first read this study, I focused on how successfully Zara's business model had been. At the time, I didn't realize that Zara's business model, which is used by other fast-fashion brands as well, could have devastating environmental and social impacts. But in the years that followed, I discovered that this profitable business model has awful repercussions.

Following is an overview of how the fast-fashion business model operates and can negatively impact the environment and its workers. Figure 3-1 provides a visual of this process.

>> **Fast replication/development of fashion trends:** Fast-fashion companies develop or replicate trends in a short time frame. They get inspiration from high-end runway looks, indie designers, or celebrities. They are able to do this

because fashion, unlike music, is not protected by copyright laws. Brands are sued a lot, but for the most part, nothing happens.

- **>> Fast on-demand manufacturing:** In order to have inventory available quickly for the market, manufacturing has to be fast. Garments need to be out of the factory in as little as two or three weeks. The work is mostly done overseas in low-cost countries, where workers work arduous hours and under terrible conditions to meet deadlines.

- **>> Mass production:** Fast fashion provides cheaper clothes. This is only economically viable through economies of scale, so they have to mass produce. For example, I once searched the Fashion Nova website for pink dresses and found a whopping 959 dresses!

- **>> High profit margins:** To achieve high profit margins, sales must be high and costs super low. This is why garment workers are paid low wages and clothes are made from lower-quality fabric.

- **>> Low-cost manufacturing:** A lot of the manufacturing is done outside the United States and western Europe, in countries that are relatively low-cost, such as China, Bangladesh, Cambodia, Vietnam, and India, to maximize profit. Wages paid to workers in these low-cost countries tend to be so low that the workers can barely afford what they need to survive (see "Taking a toll on garment workers"). Even when fast fashion brands manufacture in the United States or other western countries, they tend to look for opportunities to pay the lowest possible wages.

Costing more than you may think

Fast fashion is marketed as inexpensive and accessible. At the register it may seem inexpensive, but in the long run it can be quite wasteful and more expensive. Moreover, some super-popular fast-fashion brands like Zara aren't even that inexpensive, in my opinion.

REMEMBER

Fast-fashion brands produce and market runway or designer-inspired looks for less, but they're still not always inexpensive. Items can retail for upwards of $100 but yet not be designed to last. Even worse, the garment workers receive a pittance of a wage to make the garments.

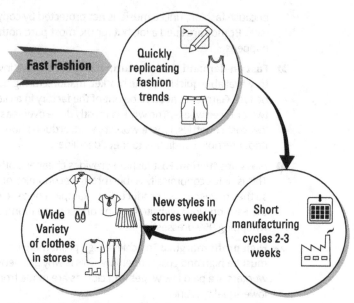

FIGURE 3-1: Fast fashion in a nutshell.

The following sections explain why fast fashion is not as inexpensive as it's claimed to be.

Higher cost per wear

Cost per wear, or CPW (discussed in more detail in Chapter 6), is key to figuring out whether a fashion purchase is worth your money. At the register you may seem to have gotten a bang for your buck, but have you? When you consider CPW, you may not have! CPW is simply the price of the item divided by the number of times you wear the item. The smaller the number, the greater your investment.

WARNING

With garments built for very short-term trends and otherwise not built to last, the CPW of fast-fashion items is much higher compared to quality garments.

To illustrate cost per wear, consider a $20 bathing suit (which is usually considered inexpensive for swimwear). Say you wear it four times, so the CPW is $5. And after four outings to the pool, the suit is faded and starting to show wear, so you have to (or want to) buy another suit and drop another $20. Now consider a quality swimsuit designed to last that costs $100 and is one that you will certainly get 25 wears out of. The CPW is $4. A frequent fast-fashion consumer only wears clothes a handful of times and is always shopping, so the CPW is always going to be higher. This example illustrates that fast fashion seems cheaper at the register, but in the long run, it's more expensive.

"More is better" psychology

When you are constantly bombarded with the marketing of a lot of stuff, you find yourself having the urge to shop more often than you need to. This is how the fast-fashion business model works. Fast-fashion brands use tactics to encourage you to shop: for example, rearranging stores, stocking often so there is always something new, focusing on trends making last year's (or week's stuff) less desirable, and promoting limited editions and drops. If you are always shopping, you are always spending money. The psychological pressure to buy more stuff creates some expensive habits.

I used to enjoy watching YouTube shopping haul videos, but when I did the math, I found that those shopping sprees add up. Some of the statistics are alarming: Fast fashion produces 100 billion items of clothing a year, with fast-fashion stores bringing new clothes every week. Today, the average American buys way more clothes than they did 30, 20, or even 10 years ago. But studies show that they wear only about 20 percent of their clothes 80 percent of the time. This means that many people spend money on clothes they aren't wearing. I don't care how cheap an item was; if you're not wearing it, that's wasting money. It shouldn't be common to find clothes with tags months or even years after you purchase them, but this is in fact quite common. Simply put, our relationship with fashion has changed, but not in a good way. It's becoming less deliberate because there is just so much fast fashion available.

Not designed to last

WARNING

Fast-fashion garments are not designed to last; the emphasis is not on longevity and quality. Fast-fashion brands aim to bring as much quantity as possible to the market at lightning speed, which does not allow them the time and space to make durable garments. Sure, you may be able buy a swimsuit for $20, but if it falls apart the first time you wear it, you'll need to keep buying more. Once I realized that I could spend just a little bit more to get my hands on timeless/evergreen pieces, which in the long run not only provides the satisfaction that comes from a quality garment but also costs less in real terms, it was an easy choice.

Taking a toll on garment workers

The fashion industry is labor-intensive, fast fashion even more so. When you hear about mass production in fashion, it's not machines and robots but a lot of human labor busy sewing, dying, cutting, and assembling. Fast fashion produces 100 billion items of clothing a year, so a lot of labor is needed. One in six people work in the fashion industry, and this is mostly women in developing nations. Fast fashion is cheap because garment workers aren't treated fairly. So how are these people being compensated for their work? Unfortunately, they're paid very low wages, exposed to unsafe working conditions, and forced to work long hours.

Earning less than a living wage

While wages may vary, for the most part, they are very low and don't constitute a living wage within the individual countries where fast-fashion brands do most of their manufacturing. For example, according to the Global Living Wage Coalition (a research and advocacy organization focused on securing living wages for working people), in 2021, the living wage in Bangladesh was $255 a month. In Vietnam, the 2020 living wage was $321 a month. (I reference Bangladesh and Vietnam because a lot of garment manufacturing is done these countries.) Unfortunately, salaries for garment workers can be as low as $100 a month.

Fast fashion brands have strong bargaining power and choose the factory that can provide the work at the least cost. Also, governments in these countries receive tax revenues from garment production, and if these governments put pressure on these brands, they just move the business to a lower-cost country. Unfortunately, if the outfit you have your eye on is inexpensive, that may mean that the people making the clothing are paid very little.

TECHNICAL STUFF

According to the Clean Clothes Campaign, a garment worker's rights advocacy organization, labor costs rarely exceeded 3 percent of the price we pay for our clothes. This means that increasing wages to a living wage wouldn't be exceptional costly for fashion brands, and it wouldn't adversely impact their profits either.

Enduring poor factory conditions

I first learned of sweat shops in a social studies class as a child. Sadly, sweatshops and labor atrocities are not a thing of the past; they have just shifted overseas to the global south. In the early '90s, Nike became infamous for manufacturing their products in sweatshops. More recently, in 2013, over a thousand people were killed as a result of poor factory conditions. (See the nearby sidebar "Tragedy in Dhaka, Bangladesh.")

When tragedy strikes, brands tend to claim that they aren't responsible because they don't own these factories and can't police what goes on there. But that disregards the fact that these brands have a lot of power — perhaps all the power. They are the clients that drive the most significant business for the owners of the factories, so they have an ability to influence conduct in positive ways.

In the fast-fashion business model, profitability is driven by extreme cost savings at the expense of worker safety and welfare. Mass production, involving workers being forced to work long shifts of 12–14 hours, typically in factories that are hot and not well ventilated, is basically standard. Additionally, many cases have been reported of women experiencing sexual assault and abuse, women who can't afford childcare sometimes bringing their kids to their unsafe workspaces, unionized workers facing intimidation, and workers generally being powerless.

TECHNICAL STUFF

Fast-fashion brands mass produce garments and usually need to work with multiple factories to meet their needs, making it more challenging to effectively audit their supply chains for worker safety. Sustainable brands, on the other hand, tend to operate on a smaller scale, working with fair-trade certified factories, and as a business practice, auditing their supply chains for worker safety. Some sustainable brands operate their own factories.

TRAGEDY IN DHAKA, BANGLADESH

On April 24, 2013, the Rana Plaza building in Dhaka, Bangladesh collapsed, killing 1,132 people and injuring 2,500 people. This building housed five garment factories that produced garments for some well-known fast fashion brands.

Apparently, the building was not safely built, and that combined with the unsafe working conditions produced this deadly result. The scenes from of the tragic event are one of the grim reminders of the human cost of fast fashion. It's not clear whether or not the companies associated with the factories operated in the building, including Inditex, the parent company of fast-fashion giant Zara, have cleaned up their act.

Being exposed to harsh chemicals

It has been widely reported that toxic chemicals like lead, PFAS, and phthalates have been found in fast-fashion brands' clothes — chemicals that are linked to brain, heart, kidney, endocrine, and reproductive harm. These chemicals get into the clothes during the manufacturing process from chemicals used in the processing of textiles; toxins also come from dyes. Consumers and workers are exposed to these chemicals. Some attention has also been drawn to farmers, those who grow the cotton used in the manufacturing of garments. Many farmers are forced to use high-yielding patented seeds to meet the high demand for cotton; these seeds don't necessarily grow well in the farmers' local environments, and the farmers are forced to use pesticides. Exposure to these chemicals has been linked to certain cancers, neurological disorders, and other chronic conditions.

REMEMBER

Fast fashion provides low-cost clothes, but the toll on workers is simply intolerable. When you see an ad for a $5 tee or $20 pair of jeans, remember this means that a worker somewhere in the world made less than a living wage and endured harsh conditions to create that item.

Adversely affecting the environment

To really get how bad fast fashion is for the environment, it's important to understand circular fashion *Circular fashion* simply means garments are circulated for as long as their value is retained and then returned safely to the earth. It's a long-term view of things, thinking about a garment's next use and how garments can be disposed of responsibly when they're no longer useable.

Fast fashion is not circular and takes a more linear approach to fashion: Raw materials are extracted, made into clothes, and then thrown away. To be fair, real efforts are made to recycle, but a lot more is not recycled. Smaller sustainable brands are doing much better by producing less, having garment takeback programs, selling preloved items, recycling old garments, using eco-friendly materials, and incorporating waste management. A linear way of doing business, especially on such a massive scale, takes its toll on the environment.

According to the World Economic Forum,

» Fashion produces 10 percent of human carbon emissions.
» The fashion industry is the second largest consumer of water.
» Eighty-five percent of all textiles end up in landfills each year.

This section elaborates on these statistics and their adverse impact on the environment.

Creating microplastics

The impacts from microplastics are super scary. *Microplastics* are tiny plastic pollution, specifically defined by the National Ocean Service as small plastic pieces, less than 5 millimeters long, which end up in our oceans where marine life mistakes them for food and ingests them.

What do microplastics have to do with fast fashion? Thirty-five percent of microplastics come from laundering synthetic garments. If you pay attention to labels, you can see that fast-fashion brands use a lot of synthetic fibers, such as nylon and polyester, that are essentially plastic and made from petroleum. Microplastics freak me out because there are many unknowns about their impact and how to reduce it, and yet they seem to be everywhere. Fish end up consuming microplastics, and scientists have even found them in human fetuses and the soil.

TIP

Don't panic and throw out your clothes made from synthetic fibers. There are solutions, like the Guppyfriend laundry bag. When washing your clothes in the washing machine, these bags trap some of the microplastics. And don't over-wash your clothes! (See Chapter 10 for tips on how to reduce microplastics in your laundry.)

TECHNICAL
STUFF

The microplastics problem is a big one, and it's going to take a lot of effort and commitment from governments and industry to fix it. As an individual, you can influence events around the edges but shouldn't get too anxious; this problem requires action from governments and industry. You can keep yourself in the loop on what is being done to address this issue by checking out non-profits like Plastic Soup Foundation or the National Oceanic and Atmospheric Administration (NOAA).

Filling landfills

Fast fashion has created a disposable fashion culture; we are throwing away so much stuff. The stats are alarming. The Ellen Macarthur Foundation estimates that the equivalent of one garbage truck of clothes is sent to landfills every minute! Once in a landfill, clothes take decades to decompose, emitting greenhouse gasses in the process. (*Greenhouse gases* contribute to climate change by trapping heat and holding it in the atmosphere.) On top of that, the clothes in landfills leach microplastics and chemicals into the ground and water.

Polluting air and water

According to the World Economic Forum, fashion production makes up 10 percent of humanity's carbon emissions. Consumers of fast fashion don't see this pollution as production is mostly overseas. Textile dyes are responsible for 20 percent of all industrial water pollution worldwide. Textile dyeing is the world's second-largest polluter of water because the water leftover from the dyeing process is often dumped into ditches, streams, or rivers. It has been widely reported that the Citarum River in Indonesia is one of the most polluted rivers. Due to wastewater from textile factories, the fish are gone, and residents are struggling with chronic illnesses.

Wasting water

Multiple sources have reported that it takes about 700 gallons (2,700 liters) of water to produce one cotton shirt. That's enough water for one person to drink at least eight cups a day for three-and-a-half years. It takes about 2,000 gallons of water to produce a pair of jeans. That's more than enough for one person to drink eight cups per day for ten years. Fast fashion is producing these items on a massive scale, so the water waste is significant.

Using unsustainable fabrics

Many fabrics used by fast-fashion brands, including conventional (not organic) cotton, polyester, and viscose, have an adverse impact on the environment.

COTTON

Cotton is a tricky fabric. Being a natural fiber, it's generally considered good, and all cotton is typically marketed as good fabric. Cotton is a versatile fabric that is used to make tees, dresses, and even denim, making it one of the most common fabrics in clothes. But conventional cotton (not organic cotton) — described by some as a dirty crop — requires a lot of pesticides and water to grow and process into fabric. Growing conventional cotton requires irrigation in addition to rainwater. Compared to linen, for example, which requires only rainwater, too much water is consumed to grow conventional cotton.

Conventional cotton seeds are mostly high-yielding seeds to meet the demand for cotton by the fashion industry, but these seeds don't do well in local environments. A lot of pesticides are required to compensate for local environments otherwise being inhospitable to the growth of conventional cotton. Conventional cotton consumes 16.1 percent of the world's insecticides and 5.7 percent of global pesticides. These chemicals are harmful to our soil and to farmers' health. Organic cotton is a better alternative to conventional cotton because it requires less water and pesticides to grow.

POLYESTER

You may be surprised how many of the garments and other fabrics you own are made from polyester or a poly blend, even those that don't remotely look like they are from polyester. As I gained more knowledge about fabrics, I was surprised to find that my woolly-looking teddy coat, my old silky-looking slip dresses, and even some of my bedsheets are made from polyester. *Polyester* is a new fabric from the 1940s. It's made from oil, so it's essentially a form of plastic. It has become the most frequently used fabric because it's relatively cheap and is not subject to price and availability fluctuations like cotton.

It is not sustainable because it's a product of oil and it is common knowledge that the petrochemical industry is the most polluting industry. Polyester isn't biodegradable either; once it's in landfills it takes 500 years–plus to decompose. Polyester also sheds microplastics when laundered. See the earlier section "Creating microplastics" for more on this topic.

Other synthetic fibers that are made from oil and have similar environmental concerns are nylon and Lycra (spandex). But alternatives exist. (Turn to Chapter 5 for more information on recycled synthetics.)

VISCOSE

Viscose, also known as rayon, mimics silk; in fact, people regularly mistake viscose for silk. *Viscose* is a fabric made from natural fibers, like cellulose of wood pulp, but as with cotton, high demand from the fashion industry has led to poor environmental practices such as deforestation.

Moreover, the chemicals required to break down cellulose into fabric, such as carbon disulfide, can be quite toxic. The runoff from these chemicals pollutes rivers and has been linked to occupational exposure to cancers and nervous system disorders. Eco-friendly alternative Tencel (discussed in Chapter 5) is made from wood from responsibly/sustainably managed forests, and a closed-loop chemical process is used, meaning that no chemicals escape into water and the environment.

Spotting Fast Fashion

You know what fast fashion is and the issues it causes (if not, see the earlier section "Identifying the Real Cost of Fast Fashion"), but maybe you aren't sure whether a brand you like is part of the fast-fashion problem. This section explains how to spot a fast-fashion brand — so that you can avoid it, of course!

There are renowned fast-fashion brands for which name association alone is typically sufficient. You can discover how to spot clothes made by those brands and instantly associate them with fast fashion. Here, I provide a list of some of those brands and point out some of the telltale signs of fast fashion.

Identifying popular fast-fashion brands

Here I share a few well-known examples of fast-fashion brands. You may have heard of them, or even own their clothes, but didn't know that they are part of the fast-fashion problem.

REMEMBER

This list is not designed to shame anyone away from patronizing these brands; my mission in writing this book is to inspire you to make sustainable fashion choices.

>> **Fashion Nova:** This brand is relatively new in the fashion industry and has been hugely successful. It has scooped numerous celebrity endorsements, and social media patronage is off the charts. Fashion Nova is described as ultra-fast fashion, with 600 to 900 new styles dropping every week.

>> **H&M:** H&M is also a well-known fast-fashion brand. It's a Swedish brand with retail locations across the globe in over 70 countries. It's popular for its trendy, inexpensive fashion.

>> **Nike:** Nike is probably one of the largest athletic-wear brands. Most of us, including myself, have a pair of Nike shoes. In the 1990s, Nike was involved in a sweatshop scandal and was the target of protests at the 1992 Barcelona Olympics.

>> **Shein:** Shein is also ultra-fast fashion and is extremely popular for its inexpensive, trendy fashion. Shein became the most downloaded app in the United States in 2022.

>> **Zara:** I expect some backlash for mentioning Zara here because it's an insanely popular brand. Zara pretty much popularized fast fashion. Zara brings a tremendous amount of new clothes into its stores every week, with essentially 52 seasons.

TIP

Keep in mind these aren't the only fast fashion brands out there. Once you have deep understanding of the differences between fast fashion and sustainable fashion, you'll be able to spot more fast fashion brands.

REMEMBER

Low costs isn't the only sign that a brand sells fast fashion. In fact, there're fast-fashion brands that are relatively expensive. If you want to find out whether a specific brand is fast fashion or not, do some research. You can also make the call yourself by evaluating the brand's products, website, and culture.

Spotting telltale signs that a brand is fast fashion

Before you buy that cute outfit, determine whether the company that produced it is part of the fast-fashion problem. Fast-fashion brands may not tell you outright what camp they belong to, but you can certainly pick up on some clues. Some brands are known to be fast fashion (see the preceding section "Identifying popular fast-fashion brands"). Others may be less obvious. To identify the less obvious players, consider some telltale signs:

>> **New stock all the time:** When you shop at sustainable or slow-fashion brands, you notice significantly fewer drops and restocks (see Chapter 5 more info). Fast-fashion brands, on the other hand, have new stuff all the time because they are mass-producing clothes.

>> **Brands at your local mall (especially trendy ones):** This may seem like over-generalization because unquestionably, there are some smaller, sustainable brands at malls, but most brands at local malls are skewed toward fast fashion.

>> **Bargain pricing and frequent sales and promotions:** Fast-fashion brands almost always have bargain prices and nearly constant sales because mass production gives them economies of scale. If jeans retail at approximately $20 or tees retail at around $5, more likely than not, that's a fast-fashion brand.

>> **Trendy items:** Fast-fashion brands tend to have the trendiest clothes. Their business model is based on offering trendy clothes so a customer can come back often to shop ever newer trends. Clearly, there can be such a thing as too much choice! That is what fast fashion does — provides too much, needless choice. You really don't need several shopping hauls every season to express your style. There just aren't enough days to wear all these clothes.

>> **Poor fabric quality:** When you shop sustainable brands, you notice a lot more transparency regarding sourcing and

that they clearly take pride in the quality of their fabrics. Fast-fashion brands use a lot of synthetic materials like polyester because of the low prices and versatility of these types of fabrics. These fabrics are not good quality and are also harmful to the environment (see the section "Adversely affecting the environment"). Beware of blended fabrics. For example, something may be marketed as cotton yet be a cotton/polyester blend, and often linen won't be 100 percent linen.

>> **Brands featured on YouTube shopping hauls:** Although there are exceptions, most of the brands featured on social media shopping hauls are fast-fashion brands. A shopping haul typically consists of fashion garments that are bought from a single retailer, are currently in the store, and are cheap.

>> **Quality and fit issues:** When garments are mass-produced for style and not longevity, quality and fit issues are more prevalent. Getting a few of those trendy pieces that just don't fit quite right is a lived experience of many. Maybe the chest is too tight, the pockets aren't functional (or they're nonexistent), the sleeves are too tight, and so on. While this can happen even with sustainable brands, these brands tend to produce small batches, so they can fix such issues for subsequent batches; in contrast, when clothes that have been mass-produced with issues end up in the stores, they tend to be returned and end up in landfills.

I bought palazzo pants from a fast-fashion brand because they looked cute, but a lot was wrong with the pants! The pockets were too long and yet visible so they just looked awkward on me, and nothing could fit in the pockets without bulging out. I kept the pants but struggled to ever wear them confidently.

REMEMBER

Cheapness is not the only attribute that makes a brand unethical or unsustainable. There are some higher-end brands that may not fit in the fast-fashion category but yet have questionable labor and environmental practices. Fashion has always had trouble operating ethically, but fast fashion flaunts the unethical practices on a grander scale. So any middle-of-the-fairway-type brands must work on fixing their supply chain and environmental practices, which are invariably problematic.

WARNING

Just because a brand is made in the United States, the United Kingdom, or the Western world does not always mean the brand is paying fair wages. In 2020, Boohoo was under modern slavery investigations for paying workers 3.50 pounds an hour at a Leicester factory, which is way below a minimum wage or a living wage in the United Kingdom.

Moving Away from Fast Fashion and Toward Sustainability

Equipped with all the information regarding the adverse environmental and social impacts of fast fashion, you may have given serious thought to letting it go but found yourself wondering what you can do when it appears that all the stores or brands that market to you or are in neighborhood malls are fast fashion. This section provides some guidance for getting through your breakup with fast fashion.

I'm not trying to shame you if you buy clothes from fast-fashion brands. Most people are frequent fast-fashion consumers! What matters is that you consider the cons of fast fashion the next time you go shopping and take small steps toward becoming a sustainability fashionista.

WARNING

All the negative information you have heard and read about fast fashion may cause you to want to throw your fast-fashion clothes away, but don't do so because they will likely end up in landfills, compounding the problem; you want to keep your clothes — including fast fashion — in use for as long as possible.

A lot of your closet is probably fast fashion. Fast fashion is the most available fashion on the market for new clothes. Fast fashion is problematic (see the earlier section "Identifying the Real Cost of Fast Fashion" for details), but it's important to prolong the life of the fast fashion you already have. Eighty-five percent of textiles end up in landfills, so prolonging the life of your clothes is super important.

TIP

Treat your fast-fashion clothes as you treat your delicate clothes. Your fast fashion items probably aren't made from the strongest of fabrics or stitching. Wash them by hand, wash them less (as they shed microplastics too!), and air-dry them to help them last longer. Mend them and remove stains in a timely manner. Treat them the same way you treat special garments. By doing so, you are preserving them for longer use. For more advice on prolonging the life of your clothes, check out Chapters 10 and 11.

Confronting Greenwashing

If it feels too good to be true from a fast fashion brand, it could be greenwashing.

Fast-fashion brands do a lot of greenwashing. *Greenwashing* is when a brand exaggerates or flat-out lies about its sustainability claims, conveying a false impression that a company or product is environmentally friendly. This section tells you more about this all-too-common issue.

Taking a peek at sustainability

Greenwashing capitalizes on the growing desire by consumers for eco-friendly products and services. This deceptive practice is no doubt unethical, as it can falsely influence a purchase decision and violates consumer protection laws. Making you think your purchase is earth-friendly when it's not is unfair.

WARNING

Changing Markets Foundation, a sustainability non-government organization (NGO), studied the websites of 12 European fast-fashion brands, including ASOS, H&M, Zara, and Boohoo, and found that 60 percent of the environmental claims were unsubstantiated. These stats are debatable, but greenwashing does occur and is pretty widespread.

To understand greenwashing and be able to call it out, you need to have a good understanding of what are and aren't sustainable fashion practices. See Chapter 5 for details of the attributes of sustainable fashion brands. Key aspects of sustainable fashion include the following:

>> **Less production:** Sustainable brands produce fewer items. Fast fashion has an overproduction problem. The fashion industry is producing 100 billion garments annually.

>> **Living wages:** A brand that pays living wages and is not focused on maximizing profits by paying the lowest possible wages generally tends to be committed to sustainability.

>> **Low waste or zero waste practices:** Sustainable brands work hard to reduce waste as much as possible. They do this in many ways, such using less water and fabric. Many sustainable brands use the left-over fabric to make other usable products.

>> **Quality eco-friendly fabrics:** Sustainable brands typically use eco-friendly fabrics like organic linen, recycled cotton, or recycled wool.

REMEMBER

A brand would have to achieve most of the preceding bullet points for it to qualify to be described as sustainable; a brand's claim to being sustainable isn't properly anchored if it just does one or two things that can be characterized as attributes of sustainability. You have probably seen a lot of marketing around sustainable jeans, which I applaud because making denim is very water-intensive, but using less water alone doesn't make a brand sustainable.

Spotting greenwashing

If you want to shop sustainably, you should steer clear of any deceitful greenwashing practices (fast fashion in disguise). Here are some tips to help you spot greenwashing so you can avoid it.

>> **Sustainable or eco-conscious lines, but everything else is not sustainable:** Most of the major fast-fashion players have these lines, including H&M's Conscious and Zara's Join Life. Gap and Banana Republic also have eco-conscious lines. These lines represent a small percentage of these brands' inventory, and in any case, they mostly focus on fabrics with no mention of labor practices. While the styles of these eco-conscious lines are relatively good, in my opinion, these lines don't measure up to the best brands' collections.

>> **Impressive-sounding initiatives that have no impact on supply chain:** These initiatives can include energy use at stores or headquarters, and labels made from recycled paper. Another example is the use of paper bags instead of plastic, which, while commendable, is already required by law in some countries or states. Focusing on what consumers see rather than fixing what they don't see (for example, fixing endemic problems with their supply chains) is not a real solution.

>> **Lofty goals and targets:** There are no set requirements for brands to achieve or to adhere to with regards to sustainability. Brands are free to set targets for their environmental impact that are comfortable to achieve. Many brands set lofty greenhouse gas emission reduction targets as part of *COP26* (the 26th United Nations Climate Change Conference of the Parties), but so far very little evidence indicates that they will actually meet these goals. You shouldn't evaluate brands based on these publicly announced targets. In fact, the targets can be so lofty, yet very little verifiable evidence exists to show that they are being pursued. The publicity associated with announcing such targets can be a form of greenwashing.

>> **Recycling bins at stores:** When I started my sustainable fashion journey, I thought H&M was a sustainable brand because of the recycling bins at their stores. But there is no clear, public information on what happens to the clothes put into these bins. Customers aren't told whether the recycled clothes are made into new fabrics or made into other products.

>> **Payment of minimum wage versus living wage:** Payment of minimum wage is a requirement of applicable law in the place brands operate; you should remember that a minimum wage is often not a living wage. A living wage is the amount an individual or family would need to avoid living in poverty.

>> **Planting trees for your purchases (but no sustainable practices otherwise):** We can all agree that we need more trees, but planting trees for every purchase does not make a brand sustainable. Planting trees does not offset river pollution and unfair labor practices. It's really a gimmick to show that a brand cares about doing right.

REMEMBER

Please note that are some sustainable brands out there, like TenTree, that check all sustainability boxes and plant trees when purchases are made. So don't rush to assume all tree planting is greenwashing. It depends on the brand.

>> **Use of buzzwords:** Claims involving buzzwords like "good for the earth," "earth-friendly," "natural fibers," "green," and so on can be — and often are — just made up because no standards exist to constitute their validity. Also beware

certifications by organizations without any real repute. Not all certifications are legitimate; if you see one, do a Google search to make sure it's not made up.

Chapter 5 includes information on some commonly used, legitimate certifications. Examples include GOTS (Global Organic Textile Standard) and Fair Trade Certified.

GREENWASHING IS FACING REGULATORY ACTION

TECHNICAL STUFF

The U.S. Securities and Exchange Commission (SEC) is taking regulatory action against listed companies that make false or misleading claims about their sustainability practices. On March 21, 2022, the SEC proposed disclosure requirements to standardize the climate-related information that listed companies provide to investors and the public. The SEC followed up with another proposal on May 25, 2022, which, if finalized, will require certain investment managers and funds to

- Include specific disclosures regarding ESG (Environmental Social Governance) strategies in fund prospectuses, annual reports, and adviser brochures
- Implement a form of ESG disclosure that allows investors to compare the ESG information
- Disclose the greenhouse gas emissions of their investments

This is a big deal. The risk of SEC action would restrain big companies from flat-out lying about their sustainability practices. This is likely to reduce the proliferation of greenwashing, but you should remain vigilant. Big private companies that don't face the risk of SEC action will still have the incentive to engage in greenwashing, so it is important to be able to identify the greenwashing red flags.

Chapter **4**

Shifting to a Sustainable Fashion Mindset

S hifting to a sustainable fashion mindset requires knowledge and a little willpower. Yes, a little willpower because the fashion that is most accessible (or certainly considered more accessible) is fast fashion. *Fast fashion* means fast, high-volume, trendy, and inexpensive fashion. Fast fashion emphasizes making fashion trends available to consumers quickly and cheaply. Trendy, colorful fashion, at unbeatable low prices, can be tempting. Even after you have gained an appreciation of the negative impacts of fast fashion on the environment and fast fashion's unethical labor practices, you may still struggle with how you transition away from fast fashion. But you've got this! Don't be too hard on yourself; building more sustainable shopping habits takes time. What matters is that you take that first step toward sustainability!

This chapter guides you in staying motivated on your sustainable path, as well as navigating and resisting fast-fashion temptation, and some other options for you to consider to help reduce how much you shop.

Shopping as a Sustainable Fashion Consumer

Shopping sustainably in a fast-fashion-dominated world certainly can be challenging. It's normal to be tempted to feel like you are missing out, making your shopping even more complicated for you. Everywhere you turn — the malls, your inbox, social media feeds, and so forth — you see fast fashion, so you need to filter that out and actively seek out sustainable fashion. Fast fashion has trendy styles, but it's not the only way to be stylish. Plus, protecting Mother Earth should be incentive enough to shop sustainably. From my personal experience, shopping sustainably has been liberating; I'm not swayed by trends and the need to always be on top of what's trending (but you can shop trends more sustainably; see "Feeding the Trend Monster" later in this chapter). In general, I've spent less on fashion. Moreover, I think and feel more stylish than I have ever been and love my clothes more because I bought them more intentionally.

As a sustainable fashion consumer, you should focus on the following as general guiding principles:

>> Shop *intentionally.* This means buying clothes and shoes that you need, that fit your personal style, and that you can see yourself wearing long term.

>> Don't shop trends unless you really, truly like them. It's okay to let some trends slip by.

>> Shop from sustainable sources, sustainable brands, and secondhand whenever you can.

TIP

While I advocate thrifting and shopping sustainable brands, this may not be possible all the time. Even if you end up shopping from a brand that isn't very sustainable, make sure you always shop intentionally.

Read on for practical pointers on what you can do starting today to shift to more sustainable shopping habits.

Avoiding Impulse Buys

You might have some clothes in your closet that you've never worn. These are likely clothes that were impulse buys.

Before I started my sustainable fashion journey, I bought clothes and accessories from fast-fashion brands. I loved outlet malls and bought stuff from well-known brands that I didn't really like, just because the stuff was discounted and was from a popular brand. As you build better sustainable shopping habits, you need to try to resist impulsive shopping. Avoid impulse buys by taking a moment to reflect on whether you really need to buy an item.

REMEMBER

Unless you have only the clothes on your back, shopping should never really be super urgent. Fast fashion has created a "grab stuff before it's gone" mentality, an artificial urgency to shop for clothes.

So how do you figure out whether you really need that elegant ensemble? The overriding guiding principle should be that every item of clothing you buy should have the potential to be worn 30 times. (Chapter 6 explains this 30-wears idea in more detail.) To determine whether the item you've got your eye on makes the cut, ask yourself these questions:

>> Do I really need the item I'm about to buy? Am I buying it just because it's on sale?

>> Do I have something similar?

>> Where will I wear this outfit? Does it fit my lifestyle, or will it collect dust in my closet because I have nowhere to wear it?

>> Do I have shoes to match it? Do I need to wear a special bra? Think practically.

>> Does it feel comfortable? You can only wear clothes multiple times if you are comfortable wearing them.

>> Can I wear it in different ways? Is it versatile?

COPING WITH A SHOPPING ADDICTION

Shopping addictions or compulsive shopping has been described as a preoccupation with purchasing products and spending money.

This mental health issue affects many people worldwide. Compulsive shopping or shopping addiction is said to cause financial debt and reduced quality of life. If you think you have a shopping addiction, consider talking to a therapist or joining support groups.

Also, as a sustainable fashion consumer, you can dig deeper and examine clothes through sustainability and ethical lenses. Consider the following factors:

>> **Who made the clothes?** Dig deeper to find out whether the brand has an ethical supply chain. Have workers been compensated fairly? Look for certifications like Fair Trade Certified, which certifies that clothes were made in a fair-trade factory, meaning that workers received fair wages and worked under good working conditions. Check out Chapter 5 for more guidance on certifications.

>> **What are my clothes made from?** Dig deeper to find out what fabrics are used and if those fabrics are sustainable. The most sustainable fabrics are organic natural fabrics, with organic linen, organic hemp, and recycled cotton among the most sustainable fabrics. (To find out more about sustainable fabrics, check out Chapter 5.)

Use shopping lists

A great way for you to shop sustainably is to make shopping lists and do your best to stick to them. Buy only what you need. Making your list is easy but you need to put some time into it, so you are getting what you really need and like.

Determining what you really need or want to buy

A good shopping list requires some groundwork. First you should check your closet to see what you already have. Auditing your wardrobe means knowing what you have and what has worked for you. You don't want to buy stuff that you already have or buy things that haven't worked for you. This helps you as you plan your list. (Chapter 2 guides you through auditing your closet.)

Getting fashion inspiration

If you need some inspiration. Pinterest is a great place for visual inspiration and can double as a mood board if you save the pins you like. The mood board will serve as a digital collage of images for your ideas that you can refer back to when needed. I get a lot of inspiration from casually watching people and noting how they put outfits together. I also get some inspiration from social media. If you read magazines, flip through some of those; you can also take pictures of mannequins in stores. If you are considering *capsules* (wardrobes with selections of interchangeable clothes that complement each other), look up capsule wardrobe essentials and check out Chapter 6 for some ideas on what you need to create your capsule wardrobe.

WARNING

If you have a shopping addiction, you might find looking at photos of outfits on social media to be triggering. Do what's best for you. That might mean you need to ignore or block all fashion content from your social media feed.

TIP

Check your closet to see if you have anything similar to what you've saved to your mood board. You may be lucky and find that you can shop your closet to create the look you're going for.

Writing out your list

I organize my list into two categories: my "needs" and my "nice-to-haves." The needs are foundational pieces that work well for many outfits. Think black pants, button-up shirts, layering pieces, or a winter coat. The nice-to-haves have less priority and are great items to thrift — for example, an extra bag in a new color, just to add color to your outfits.

Doing some research

Now that you've made a shopping list, it's time to find out where to get the stuff on the list, focusing on quality (and of course your budget). You shouldn't be rushing to shop. Look at sustainable fashion directories, like Good on You, for sustainable brands; look at reviews; and then go to the store and try on clothes to see how they feel. Chapter 13 includes a short-list of great sustainable clothing brands.

TIP

Keep your list handy, preferably on a notes app on your smartphone (as you'll usually have your phone with you), so if you're out and about and are tempted to buy something, you can check your list to determine whether you really need it.

Take your time

Practice being a slow shopper; take time to think about items you're considering buying. If you're shopping online, pin them to a Pinterest board or save your searches. Then, come back to them later.

If you're shopping in person, take the time to try on the item. If possible, go when stores are not too busy, so you can shop more leisurely. Ask the store to hold your purchases, go out for a coffee, and think about whether you want to go through with the purchase.

Phone a friend (a practical friend!) and ask for their opinion. My sister texts me whenever she goes shopping and sends a picture of what she's thinking about buying. I ask her for information on the price, the brand, the fabric, and where she will wear it. These questions help her determine whether buying the item is the right choice.

TECHNICAL
STUFF

Here is a-not-so-fun fact: A lot of that stuff that people are rushing for ends up on resale or returned. According to *Forbes*, Black Friday sales returns are estimated at about 30 percent or even up to 50 percent for some brands.

On the flip side, avoid shopping with that friend or family member who encourages impulse purchases. You may love them, but they'll probably only get you into shopping trouble.

Being Trendy and Sustainable

Shopping sustainably doesn't have to mean missing out on trends. Fashion is self-expression, and if a trend speaks to you, go for it. But you'll find more satisfaction as a sustainable shopper if the clothes' quality is such that you will wear the clothes long term, even as what's considered trendy evolves. That's the catch — it forces you to reflect on whether you are just going with the flow or really like the trend you're shopping.

So, if you decide to shop a particular trend, there's some good news for you: Trends tend to be cyclical, meaning it's likely that clothes that fit with the current trend are already in circulation somewhere (meaning these clothes likely already exist and you don't buy recently created items; they could even already be in your closet, in the thrift store, or on resale sites). What does that mean? It means you don't have to buy a new item from a fast-fashion brand to get the same trendy look. The thrift store may have what you need.

Trends can simply be rearrangements of what you already have in your closet. I go to SoHo often, which is like the fashion capital of New York City. And for fun, I take pictures of the mannequins and then try to re-create those looks with what I already own.

REMEMBER

Being a sustainable fashion shopper means taking a longer-term view of your clothing purchases and consuming trends judiciously.

Avoiding Temptation

Temptation to shop and shop 'til you drop is real, but there some ways you can navigate it. In this section, I give you some tips to help you remain steadfast in your efforts to shop intentionally and from more sustainable sources.

REMEMBER

There is a limit to the number of cute clothes you need in your closet. You probably have enough so that cute dress that's tempting you isn't a necessary purchase.

You're probably bombarded with ads from fast fashion, and shopping hauls from social media influencers on TikTok, YouTube, and Instagram, as I am. Clever marketing and good photography can tempt you to buy things that you don't need, like clothes or accessories from companies that aren't sustainable, which you definitely don't need.

TECHNICAL STUFF

I looked at TikTok hashtags and they're fast-fashion heavy. For example, #shein (a fast-fashion brand) has over 40 billion posts, #sheinhaul over 7 billion, all of which serve as an indication of how media is skewed toward fast fashion.

Detoxing your social media and inbox

Good places to start to reduce temptations are your inbox and your social media feeds. It's likely that most of what you see on social media is *not* sustainable fashion content, meaning that you need to filter out the fast fashion. Unfollow the accounts that promote frivolous spending, especially the ones that are doing endless ultra-fast-fashion hauls from brands like Shein or Fashion Nova. Anyone spending $1,000 for boxes and boxes of cheap clothes that they plan to wear once should not influence you to buy fast-fashion clothes merely because they provide an affiliate code; instead, you should seriously consider unfollowing such accounts.

Another place to detox is your inbox. Unsubscribe from those fast-fashion marketing emails, which can be tempting. Some may even send you special discount codes, saying that they miss you and inviting you to come back and shop. They don't miss you. They miss your money, and it's a trap. Don't give in!

TIP

Diversify your social media feed. If you are a heavy fashion content consumer, reduce the fashion content you see daily and give thought to other things that bring you joy. For me, I choose home décor, comedy, and photography to supplement my interest in fashion and endeavor to balance things out.

You can also follow more thrifting or sustainable fashion bloggers. (See "Finding a sustainable fashion community" for more on how to find such bloggers.)

Train your social media feed to show you less fast fashion. When you stop liking and following such content, the algorithms will send less of this content to you. You can also delete social media apps if that is a more effective way for you to avoid temptations.

Fasting from shopping

Sometimes you just need a clean break to help yourself reset. When it comes to fashion, I find that I can reduce temptations by doing shopping fasts. A shopping fast entails committing to no-buy months, meaning you won't buy any clothes or shoes for a specified period of time. It can be one month or even three months.

For inspiration and motivation, you can join Slow Fashion Movement (www.slowfashion.global), a global social community dedicated to slow fashion, or similar communities. The Slow e-fashion movement has a "no-buy-in September" theme. Often sustainable fashion bloggers will do fun styling challenges during no-buy months to inspire followers on how to style what they already own.

Of course, shopping fasts are challenging, especially for those who spend a lot of time shopping. Here are some tips to help make shopping fasts work:

>> Schedule time for other fun activities to keep you busy.

>> Announce your fast to your shopping buddies and family. Tell them not to invite you to shop or send you shopping links.

>> Organize your closet. You may appreciate what you have or be reunited with forgotten gems.

>> If you're active on social media, join a fun styling challenge that requires you to style a few clothes in multiple ways. You'll see the potential in what you already own.

Being wary of sales

Sales are a great way to buy more expensive items or save some money, but they are also a way to buy stuff you don't need. Sales can create an urgency to buy out of *fear of missing out* (FOMO).

TIP

Ask yourself whether you would buy the item at full price or are buying it just because it's on sale. Many sales items are final sales, so you may get stuck with something you don't want.

Some sales are genuine and needed by small businesses to clear inventory or drum up sales, but sometimes sales are deceptive and aren't truly sales. You probably wonder why some brands are always on sale. Granted, there are brands big enough to offer frequent discounts, but sometimes those so-called discounts aren't really sales but tactics to make you think you're getting a good deal and must act fast.

TECHNICAL
STUFF

A *Consumer Report* article titled "When are sales too good to be true?" dated October 29, 2018, discusses instances where brands create fake sales to draw customers to shop with urgency. The list prices are designed to grossly overstate the amount of savings from purchasing items on sale. These brands also run "sales" on items that have never been sold at full price. You think you are getting a deal, but you aren't.

Finding a sustainable fashion community

Because of the way our society consumes goods (including fashion), shopping sustainably can be a pretty big lifestyle change. It's completely normal if you need some community support to keep you motivated on your sustainable path. Social media is a good place to find your sustainable fashion community. I have built a community with people halfway around the world, whom I continue to learn from and have become very friendly with. There are engaged communities on Instagram and Facebook. You should follow more sustainable fashion bloggers and thrifted style bloggers. You can easily find them using relatable hashtags like #sustainablefashionblogger, #thriftedstyle, #slowfashionbloggers, and many more. You can also join relevant local Facebook groups.

Follow sustainable brands. I have built some relationships with small brands and have interacted with some of the owners online and discovered so much about their businesses and processes. Because they are small businesses, I find them to be approachable and responsive.

Taking Pride in Repeating Outfits

For some people, it's important to wear something different every day, meaning they don't repeat outfits. Maybe you avoid repeating outfits within a week or a few months. But if you are someone who never repeats an outfit, it's safe to say you own more clothes than you need.

There isn't always (and really shouldn't be) a stigma around repeating outfits. When you repeat outfits, you find yourself shopping much less. Taking pride in repeating outfits means wearing them more than once in a short period of time (at times more than once within the same week) and not feeling any shame about it. Social media trends disfavor being seen in the same outfit twice, which is unfortunate.

WARNING

Subscription shopping services offer members monthly perks or discounts on the new styles they drop every week, normalizing frivolous clothes and shoe shopping, and making it easy to have fresh outfits all the time. This method of shopping is unsustainable and should be avoided.

Let's face it: There's nothing earth shattering about repeating outfits; many people still consider it a quite normal thing to do. The problem is just that social media and fast-fashion trends have bombarded us with an avalanche of new, cheap, trendy items, causing many of us to shun repeating outfits. Ultimately, your journey is personal, and no one really cares about your choice to repeat outfits. Moreover, you are in good company if you choose to proudly repeat your outfits. You may be familiar with the Y2K TV show *Lizzie McGuire* and the infamous episode in which a bully tells Lizzie, "You are an outfit repeater!" Lizzie responds, "Maybe I'm an outfit repeater, but you're an outfit rememberer, which is just as pathetic."

TIP

Here are some tips to help you confidently repeat outfits:

>> **Change your shoes and accessories.** This is a super-easy way to transform an outfit for a new look.

>> **Change your layering pieces.** Think blazers, sweaters, and coats.

>> **Change up your hair or makeup.** Even small things like this can change up a look.

>> **Love the clothes you have.** Buy clothes that work for you. It's easier to repeat clothes that you love.

>> **Create a capsule wardrobe.** (See Chapter 6 for details.) A capsule is a selection of interchangeable clothes that complement each other and that the owner loves to wear. With a capsule, it's easy to repeat a few clothes by creating multiple looks from the complementary pieces.

>> **Ignore the outfit rememberers!** Repeat to your heart's content.

2

Purchasing Sustainable Fashion Items

Discover what sustainable fashion looks like.

Start shopping mindfully so that you purchase great clothes you actually wear.

IN THIS CHAPTER

» Defining sustainability and debunking misconceptions

» Recognizing the cornerstones of sustainable fashion

» Getting a feel for sustainable fabrics

» Evaluating the benefits of sustainable fashion

» Finding great sustainable brands all on your own

Chapter **5**

What Makes a Brand Sustainable?

What makes a brand sustainable? This question cannot be answered just by looking at glossy mission statements or publicly stated commitments around sustainability (although those are not unimportant). You have to consider how a brand operates. Brands must be judged by their deeds, not their words. What makes a brand sustainable is a combination of actions, and to be clear, there is no one-size-fits-all. A big, established brand that already has a larger carbon footprint needs to take many more actions (relative to smaller brands) for it to truthfully claim to be sustainable.

In this chapter, I call out the characteristics of a sustainable fashion brand. A brand must take certain actions and maintain certain procedures to truly be considered sustainable. This chapter provides you with the tools to identify sustainable brands on your own and explains why spending some time and effort (and money) on finding sustainable fashion is worthwhile.

Refuting Some Misconceptions about Sustainable Fashion

There is not necessarily consensus in all corners regarding what *sustainability* means for fashion. Some definitions of sustainable fashion focus solely on the environmental aspect, but I think, and many others agree, that a brand can't be sustainable without ethical labor practices. In very simple terms, sustainable fashion is fashion that is made in a way that is good for the environment *and* people. So, the better question when you are evaluating a brand is whether it is eco-friendly and people-friendly. If a brand's deeds qualify it as eco-friendly, and it is also verifiably people-friendly, then it's proper to consider it a sustainable brand.

In the last several years, sustainable brands have progressed by leaps and bounds, gaining market share in part because conscious consumers are choosing them and in part because they are making smart business decisions around positioning themselves in the market. The rate of adoption of sustainable fashion has steadily risen every year and is expected to continue to grow.

A common misconception is that sustainable fashion is boring. I can confidently tell you that there is no truth at all to that notion. Sustainable fashion comes in many styles and colors, and sustainable brands offer cute, timeless, and well-made fashions in many styles and colors. My prettiest clothes are sustainable fashion!

TIP

If you're looking to see the evidence for yourself, look up #sustainablefashion on social media. You'll find plenty of great inspiration. Not sure what accounts to follow? You can start with my Instagram account (Mspaulapresents).

Another common misconception is that sustainable fashion is really expensive. The reality is that sustainable fashion allows us to reset fashion back to how it has traditionally been produced and consumed: that is, owning fewer items that are designed to last versus the overconsumption of almost single-wear, disposable clothes that are the lifeblood of fast fashion. Sustainable fashion is a better investment because its quality and durability mean you can get more wear out of items without spending more money.

WARNING

The sizing of sustainable fashion clothing brands is not yet as inclusive as it should be. In Chapter 13, I provide some examples of size-inclusive sustainable brands, but unfortunately, not enough sustainable brands offer inclusive sizing.

Looking at Sustainable Business Practices

The term *sustainable business practices* is used in this book to describe business practices that are both people- and earth-friendly. *Earth-friendly*, which is used interchangeably with sustainable and eco-friendly, describes business practices that are focused on the least consumption of natural resources such as water. Such practices also reduce waste pollution and emissions that are harmful to the climate. *People-friendly*, on the other hand, describes business practices focused on paying farmers and factory workers a living wage and providing safe working conditions.

A lot of industries, including the fast-fashion industry, take a linear approach to business, extract resources, and make products at the lowest cost possible, thereby maximizing their profits. Maximizing profits usually entails a disinterest in how products are consumed and disposed; often both the consumption and/or disposal is not done responsibly. It's an extract–make–throw-away business model. A sustainable approach, on the other hand, is more circular and encompasses mindful extraction of resources, mindful manufacturing, and mindful or conscious profit-making — making profits but still being fair to workers throughout the supply chain. It also entails thinking about a product's entire lifespan, including how it will be disposed. Circular in this context focuses on the concept of circular fashion, which involves using and circulating clothes responsibly and effectively in society for as long as possible, disposing of them only when they are no longer fit for use. To this end, some sustainable brands offer ways to sell your preloved garments bought from them or even repair your clothes.

WARNING

So-called eco-collections or eco-conscious lines of fast-fashion brands are not sustainable fashion. These fashion lines are usually guilty of *greenwashing*, which is when brands exaggerate or fabricate stories about their sustainability initiatives. (Chapter 3 explains this concept in more detail.) Sustainability is not about having a few clothes made from recycled bottles; yes, that is a step in the right direction but really a drop in the bucket. What is needed is far more fundamental: a reworking of entire supply chains to be sustainable and ethical.

Of course, that all sounds pretty bad. But don't panic. There are other ways to run a fashion business. The sustainable fashion industry has demonstrated that profitability, mindfulness, and fairness can co-exist. The following sections outline the business practices that make a fashion line sustainable.

Sustainable environmental practices

The fashion industry is polluting our air, water, and land. The scariest part of fashion-related pollution is that most of the damage has been done in the last 20 years, attributable primarily to the rise of fast fashion. (For more information on how and why this is happening, check out Chapter 3.)

Thankfully, sustainable brands are leading the way to a more sustainable fashion future, and I hope they can provide a blueprint for the whole industry. In this section, I explain some environmental best practices for the fashion industry, not only to help you understand them and their impact but also to help you appreciate how hard eco-friendly brands are working in an industry that is clearly not doing enough.

Zero- or low-waste practices

The fashion industry is extremely wasteful. It's estimated that fully 35 percent of materials in the fashion industry supply chain go to waste. Brands that engage in practices that achieve zero-waste (or a reduction) of materials in their supply chain going to waste are engaged in sustainable environmental practices. Practices that reduce or eliminate fabric waste are a major focus of sustainable brands. One way sustainable brands waste less fabric is by hand-cutting the fabric, which achieves more precision and thus less waste than machine-cutting. Such brands also use any excess fabric they may create so that it doesn't end up in landfills. For example, they make items such as totes and hair accessories from leftover fabric. Some brands use deadstock (also known as overstock, surplus, or remnant) fabric to make their pieces. These are textiles that have been discarded but are still usable.

Tonlé is an example of a brand engaging in these sustainable environmental practices. It uses high-quality deadstock, cut waste, and textiles that would otherwise end up in landfills to create new products. The brand also takes measures in-house to reduce waste. Its fabrics are hand-cut, and any defective fabric is repurposed and woven into yarn to be used for something else.

Regenerative practices

Some sustainable brands obtain their natural fabrics from sources that engage in regenerative agriculture. Agricultural activities (including those that are part of the supply chains of fashion) inevitably lead to *degeneration* (erosion, pollution, and loss of fertility) of the soil. But a growing regenerative agricultural movement is focusing on better stewardship of agricultural land and revitalization of soil nutrients, as well as removing carbon dioxide from the atmosphere. Fashion can be regenerative of the soil and soil nutrients when it supports regenerative agriculture.

Sustainable fashion brand Christy Dawn is an example of a brand engaging in regenerative fashion; it has regenerated 25 acres of depleted land in Erode, India. The brand has worked with local farmers to replenish the soil. This land is now productive again, and this is where the brand farms it cotton and sources its fabric for its farm-to-closet collection. The land is also used to process, weave, and dye the cotton using ancient and traditional methods that work in harmony with nature. All these practices are undeniably environmentally sustainable.

Use of nontoxic and eco-friendly dyes

Textile dyes became toxic with the introduction of synthetics in the 1800s. Prior to that, dyes had come from nature — from plants and insects. After the discovery of the synthetic dye mauveine in 1856, synthetic dyes began to be used on a large scale. The reactants or reagents used in the manufacture of some synthetic dyes have been found to be toxic and therefore dangerous to workers and to the animals in the waters into which wastewater from the dyeing process is discharged.

A practice associated with a brand being sustainable is the use of nontoxic and natural dyes. Natural dyes extracted from plants can be beneficial to the environment. For example, indigo, a natural dye, is extracted from a legume that is also a nitrogen-fixing plant and can replenish soil as it grows. While natural dye production can't keep pace with the current demand for dyes by the fast-fashion industry, use of natural dyes is something you can associate with sustainable brands that generally produce fewer clothes. Another sustainable alternative to synthetic dyes is low-impact dyes. These are also synthetic but are manufactured without harmful chemicals, so they're not harmful to workers nor do they produce toxic waste.

Groceries Apparel is an example of a brand that uses only non-toxic dyes from its Vegetable Dye Studio, including dyes made from pomegranate, carrot tops, onion skins, roots, bark, flowers, and real indigo.

Carbon neutrality

Another sustainable environmental practice is carbon neutrality. The fashion industry accounts for about 10 percent of global carbon emissions. This means that activities of fashion brands in the aggregate add up to this negative impact on the planet. Sustainable brands achieve carbon neutrality in two ways: First, they do so by minimizing their carbon footprints, including favoring sustainable natural fibers over synthetic fibers made from oil, smaller-scale production, and other waste-reducing practices. Second, they offset the carbon footprint they can't eliminate.

TECHNICAL STUFF

Sustainable brands can offset their shipping-related carbon emissions by purchasing carbon offsets for every package shipped. Carbon offsetting activities are activities that reduce the amount of carbon in the atmosphere, thereby offsetting carbon emissions created from other activities. Carbon offsetting activities may be certificated in the form of *carbon credits.* Carbon credits can be sold or purchased, meaning that the emitter doesn't have to conduct the carbon offsetting activity itself; the emitter can pay cash to the persons who are conducting the carbon offsetting activity, which has the added benefit of creating jobs in communities where carbon offsetting activities are undertaken. An example of a carbon offsetting activity is tree planting/afforestation, as trees capture carbon from the atmosphere.

Examples of sustainable brands that aim to achieve carbon neutrality include Stella McCartney and Two Days Off. Stella McCartney measures and reports its direct and indirect carbon emissions and works to reduce and offset them. Two Days Off, a California-based sustainable brand, is certified climate neutral, meaning that all its carbon emissions are balanced by supporting projects that absorb an equal amount of carbon.

Fashion circularity

Fashion circularity involves using and circulating clothes responsibly and effectively in society for as long as possible, only disposing of them only when they are no longer fit for use. It's a "Make, use for as long as possible, and then dispose responsibly only when it can't be used anymore" business model.

Some sustainable brands offer ways to recycle your old garments through take-back programs or selling your old garments on their secondhand marketplaces or their websites. Some offer repair services for the garments they sell. Many sustainable brands offer at least one of these options.

TAKE-BACK PROGRAMS

According to the Circular Economy Practitioner Guide, a take-back program is "an initiative organized by a manufacturer or retailer to collect used products or materials from consumers and reintroduce them into the original processing and manufacturing cycle." So, in the case of fashion, take-back programs take your old clothes and make them into new ones, and what they can't make into new clothes, they recycle responsibly. By doing this they divert clothes from landfills. Following are some examples:

>> For Days offers a program that begins with your purchase of a take-back bag from them for $20. Then you can send them your used clothes from any brand, and they are recycled into new yarn. You also receive $20 toward a purchase at For Days.

>> Girlfriend Collective recycles their old bras, leggings, and shorts into new ones. All you need to do is pay a small shipping fee, and you get $15 store credit for recycling with them.

>> Mud Jeans, a Netherlands-based denim brand, will recycle denim from any brand as long as it is at least 96 percent cotton. They take care of shipping and handling, because taking back one old pair of jeans at the purchase of a new one, at no additional cost to the customer, is part of their business model.

SECONDHAND MARKETPLACES

Face it: You may tire of your beloved sustainable pieces, or your lifestyle, body, or style may change. Some brands take this into consideration and provide services for their customers to sell their preloved items. This is super important because the average American sends about 81 pounds of textile waste to landfills every year, which underscores the need for such services.

Some sustainable brands offer secondhand marketplaces on their websites, where customers can sell preloved items from the brand. You may be familiar with Patagonia's worn wear, where you can buy used Patagonia gear and clothes. Many others, like Mara Hoffman, Eileen Fisher, tonlé, and more, have similar setups.

REPAIR SERVICES

Some sustainable brands offer repair services. A repair service keeps clothes in your closet longer and away from landfills. Finisterre and Patagonia are examples of brands that offer repair services. All you need to do is fill out a form on their website with a description of what you need fixed. You will be given an estimate of the cost, and then you mail in your clothes. Not many brands offer repair services (probably due to logistical challenges), but thankfully, there are easy repairs that you can do yourself (see Chapter 11 for how-tos), and a local tailor can help you with what you can't do.

Eco-friendly packaging

If you shop online, you may have noticed that the items you buy tend to arrive wrapped in excess plastic, airbags, or bubble wrap, and a lot of this plastic is not recyclable in most curbside recycling programs.

As online shopping continues to explode, even from sustainable brands, utilizing sustainable packaging is very important. Some sustainable brands reduce plastic use by opting for recycled and recyclable paper mailers or cardboard or reusable packaging.

Sustainable loungewear brand Mate the Label uses recycled/recyclable paper mailers or cardboard boxes. Mud Jeans uses reusable packaging made by RePack, a Finnish sustainable packaging solutions company, that you can mail back to them with free postage.

Innovations around packaging are resulting in more eco-friendly alternatives to traditional plastic, such as bioplastic. There are questions as to whether these innovations are fully sustainable, but some sustainable brands are using them. Hopefully, as these innovations get refined, these questions will be addressed and more sustainable packaging solutions will be brought into the market.

Practices that conserve and protect water

The fashion industry is very water intensive. A lot of water is used to grow raw materials like conventional cotton, which requires extensive irrigation. Furthermore, textile production uses 79 to 93 cubic meters of water annually, which is about 4 percent of all freshwater, according to the Ellen MacArthur Foundation. The fashion industry also pollutes our water. Twenty percent of water pollution is from textile dyeing (see Chapter 3 for more insight on water pollution caused by the fast fashion industry).

So sustainable brands engage in practices that minimize their own water use and pollution impact. They do this through such practices as water conservation and using nontoxic dyes.

As an example, making denim requires a lot of water. It's made from cotton, which requires a lot of water to grow, and water is also consumed in the washing and chemical processes for bleaching, dyeing, and distressing. Australian denim brand Outland Denim is an example of a brand that practices using as little water as possible. The brand uses innovative technology, including laser equipment, to cut down on the amount of water needed for washing and bleaching by up to 65 percent.

Another way a sustainable brand can reduce its water impact is through the use of low-impact dyes. These dyes require less rinsing than conventional dyes, which saves water. Additionally, low-impact dyes don't contain harmful chemicals that pollute water. TenTree, a sustainable apparel brand, shares some information on its website about how it minimizes pollution from dyes and conserves water used in the dyeing process. It uses nontoxic and natural dyes and recycles and reuses wastewater.

Transparent supply chain

Sustainable brands tend to produce limited inventory, meaning they deal with fewer factories and can more effectively track their supply chain or even own and operate their own factories. Sustainable brands that outsource production prioritize transparency and fairness by choosing to work with factories that are audited and accredited for fair labor practices. And it doesn't stop there: These brands conduct frequent audits, ask for supplier lists, and interview workers off-site for further reassurance. This provides more visibility into their supply chain and confidence that they are selling an ethical product.

REMEMBER

Transparency doesn't only give you the assurance that you are buying an ethical product but also helps you understand and appreciate the necessity for slightly higher pricing of sustainable fashion products. You pay more because everyone down the supply chain has been treated and paid fairly.

TECHNICAL STUFF

Fast-fashion brands have a transparency problem. Many conventional brands are buyers and not makers. When you go to a Zara store, for example, the clothes you see have been made in multiple factories not owned or operated by the brand. Fast-fashion brands focus on minimizing costs, so they usually don't prioritize safety and fairness for garment workers in the factories. (Chapter 3 explains the problem with fast fashion.)

When shopping for sustainable clothing, you may notice certifications attached to the labels on the clothes. These certifications guarantee that factories employ fairly compensated labor, and fabrics are nontoxic and attained from eco-friendly sources. Labels and certifications are important and provide confidence that a product is eco-friendly and ethical. Certification is not a straightforward process — a brand needs to commit to some meaningful resources to receive certification. I know many smaller sustainable brands that may not be able to gain these certifications, not because they are not sustainable but because of the complexity of the certification process.

TECHNICAL STUFF

Because smaller sustainable brands are often self-funded, and some sustainable brands operate their own factories, they often are not able to afford the costs of the certifications, especially those related to fair labor.

Here a few of the certifications you should hope to see on the labels and what they mean:

>> **GOTS:** The Global Organic Textile Standard (GOTS) is an international textile processing standard for organic fibers and includes both the social and environmental impact of the entire supply chain. Clothes with the GOTS label are certified organic, and this label also certifies that working conditions have met all International Labor Standards, United Nations Guiding Principles on Business and Human Rights (UNGPs), and Organization for Economic Cooperation and Development (OECD) standards for fair labor.

>> **Fair Trade Certified:** This is the first certification I came across; it is for fair-trade chocolate but also covers textiles. This label certifies that clothes were made in a fair-trade factory, meaning that workers received fair wages and worked under good working conditions.

>> **BLUESIGN:** Bluesign entails certification at all levels of the manufacturing process that the fabric and other inputs used have the lowest possible impact on people and the environment. This certification also certifies the safety of the dyes and any other chemicals that may be used in the manufacturing process. BLUESIGN verified fabric is nontoxic, sustainable, and ethically made.

>> **B Corporation (B Corp):** This certifies that the business has verifiably met high standards of social and environmental performance, public transparency, and balances profit and purpose. Some sustainable brands will have this certification on their websites.

>> **The Soil Association:** Certifies that every step of a clothing brand's supply chain has met environmental and social standards. The soil association looks at a brand's use of harmful chemicals, whether or not they provide safe working conditions, its efforts to reduce energy and water usage, and many more criteria.

>> **Cradle to Cradle:** This certifies the use of either natural materials that can safely return to the earth to decompose or synthetic materials that can be used over and over without downgrading their quality. This certification comes in levels, including gold, silver, and platinum, certifying each product qualitatively.

This list is by no means exhaustive; if you see a label you are not familiar with, just look it up online.

TIP

Regardless of their certification status, a brand should be transparent about both the environmental and social aspects of its supply chain, whether this is shown explicitly through its social media pages, its website, or via credible testimonials. Sustainable brand tonlé publishes a sustainability series on its website, highlighting all its practices and testimonials.

REMEMBER Certifications and labels are important, but conversations around sustainability can be more nuanced.

Ethical labor practices

The fashion industry is a labor-intensive industry; one in six people, mostly women in the developing world, work in the industry. A brand can't be sustainable fashion without doing right by garment workers! Ethical labor means that each garment worker receives a living wage and works in a safe and healthy work environment.

TECHNICAL STUFF A minimum wage is usually the bare minimum typically mandated by law; a living wage, on the other hand, means that a worker is earning enough to keep them out of poverty. (Chapter 3 further explains the difference between a living wage and minimum wage.)

Clothes made using ethically compensated labor are more expensive, but people shouldn't suffer so that our clothes are exceptionally cheap. Moreover, many sustainable brands have items that retail for under $100 and yet they pay a living wage.

Brands that qualify to be described as sustainable pay a living wage. I have heard it asked quite often: Can fashion brands afford to pay a living wage yet remain profitable? The answer, contrary to what some fast-fashion brands may want to admit, is yes. Smaller sustainable brands are being ethical and yet are still in business and are profitable. If there is a will, there is way!

Reaching for Sustainable Fabrics

To understand the importance of fabrics being sustainable, you should understand the environmental impacts of fabrics: impacts from growing the crops to make the fabrics, to manufacturing and even disposal. Unfortunately, there is no fabric that has no impact on the earth. Anything processed has a footprint, but eco-friendly fabrics have a much smaller one. Sustainable brands make significant efforts to use fabrics with less impact on the earth. Eco-friendly fabrics range from ones you may already know, like organic linen, and some innovative fabrics like Piñatex made from pineapple leaves.

In Chapter 3, I tell you about the unsustainable fabrics used by fast-fashion companies, including polyester, spandex, viscose, and conventional cotton. The impacts of these fabrics, from harmful chemicals in pesticides to over-consumption of scarce water resources, are far reaching. There are, of course, also the adverse impacts on farmers and workers who are exposed to pesticides and toxic chemicals. Because our clothes are made from fabric, fabric choices are consequential. As such, reading labels for fabric composition is really important to make sure that you're choosing sustainable fabrics.

If you've avoiding non-sustainable fabrics, you'll need to know what fabrics are sustainable (unless your disdain for fast fashion has driven you to join a nudist colony). The following sections provide some earth-friendly alternatives for clothes-wearing folks.

Natural sustainable fabrics

Not everything that is from natural sources is sustainable. For example, conventional cotton isn't sustainable and can expose people to harsh chemicals (more on that in Chapter 3). Wool and leather are natural fabrics but sometimes aren't considered to be sustainable. (See the nearby sidebar "Can wool and leather be sustainable?") But luckily for us, sustainable natural fibers are becoming more available, and there are also organizations that can certify that natural fabrics are nontoxic, fair trade, and eco-friendly. There are five natural fabrics that are known to be more sustainable than other fabrics:

>> **Organic linen:** This is one of my favorite fabrics. It's breathable and is so durable. It's one of the oldest fabrics known to humans — Egyptian mummies were wrapped in linen. Untreated natural linen is fully biodegradable. The natural linen colors are ivory, ecru, tan, and gray. When linen is grown organically with no harsh chemicals and pesticides, it's truly a sustainable fabric. It requires significantly less water

than cotton when grown in temperate climates (most linen comes from European temperate climates, in fact not all European linen will be labeled organic but is still largely sustainable). Rainwater is sufficient for growing linen, whereas cotton requires extensive irrigation. When you see an organic-linen label (whether a natural color or dyed using nontoxic eco-friendly dyes) and the fabric is made in a fair-trade certified factory, do a happy dance because you have a sustainable and durable fabric.

>> **Organic cotton:** Unlike conventional cotton, organic cotton is grown without harsh chemicals or pesticides from non-GMO seeds. This means organic cotton is safer for you and farm workers because it does not contain toxic chemicals and does not pollute the water and soil where it is grown. As you explore sustainable cotton options, you may come across organic Pima cotton, which is considered to be the highest quality cotton. Pima cotton is a long staple cotton meaning it has extra-long fibers. Extra-long fibers create softer fabric, which I can imagine would make a comfy T-shirt. Pima cotton is naturally more resistant to pilling because it's made from long fibers, meaning it is more durable. The best Pima cotton comes from Peru, where it's a native crop. Pima cotton from Peru is picked sustainably by hand because machines will destroy the long fibers. Some sustainable brands use organic Pima cotton; if you come across it, you're in luck because it's great quality cotton and there isn't that much of it. Fair Indigo uses Pima cotton for its tees.

>> **Recycled cotton:** Recycled cotton has been ranked by some as the most sustainable type of cotton. Reusing resources rather than extracting new ones is more eco-friendly as it reduces reliance on virgin resources and saves clothes from going to landfills.

Recycled cotton has been ranked the most sustainable type of cotton — even higher than organic cotton — by Made-By (a nonprofit research firm whose mission was making sustainable fashion commonplace). Their research was based on six sustainability metrics: greenhouse gas emissions; human toxicity; energy; water; eco-toxicity; and land. Regardless of ranking, reusing what we already have, if possible, is an ideal eco-friendly practice.

Recycling cotton is not without challenges. For example, the mechanical recycling process weakens the fiber, and a lot of cotton is blended with other fabrics, which can complicate recycling. But many companies are committed to navigating these challenges and are researching ways to do so.

>> **Organic hemp:** It's great to see that more and more clothes are being made from hemp. While not as common a fabric as cotton and linen, it's an old fiber dating back to ancient China BCE, where it was used for clothing and paper through early last century. Its use declined with the increase in cultivation of cotton and use of synthetic fibers. Hemp can grow almost everywhere and requires very little water and no pesticides. It grows fast and even fertilizes the soil as it grows! It's a sustainability superstar.

TECHNICAL
STUFF

Many people confuse hemp and cannabis, but they aren't the same thing. Yes, hemp is derived from the same cannabis plant, but its tetrahydrocannabinol (THC) level is extremely low — significantly lower than cannabis. THC is the cannabinoid that produces psychoactive effects. Hemp clothes have only trace amounts, less than 0.3 percent, so you won't get high!

>> **Recycled wool:** Recycling wool is not a new thing. In fact we have been recycling wool for about 200 years. Also, it's not that hard to do, and systems for wool recycling are well established. In Prato, Italy, heralded as the birthplace of textile recycling, people have been recycling wool for over 100 years. Through a mechanical process (no chemicals) wool can be pulled back down to a raw fiber state and made into new yarn. Patagonia sources over 80 percent of its wool from recycled sources, and by doing so, has been able to save 3.4 million pounds of CO_2 emissions by choosing recycled wool over virgin wool. This is impressive and reminds me to make a mental note to recycle my old knits. Rhea, a luxury Dutch knitwear brand, will recycle your wool knits and make them into new yarn, and you get a 15 percent store credit in return.

Bamboo clothing is becoming more and more popular, but many sustainability experts are on the fence regarding its eco-friendliness. At face value, it looks promising: Bamboo is fast growing, self-regenerates (meaning no replanting is required), and doesn't need any pesticides. Processing it into fabric is where it gets tricky.

CAN LEATHER AND WOOL BE SUSTAINABLE?

Leather and wool are both natural fabrics we have used since ancient times. Wool has kept people warm for centuries, and leather is undeniably durable. Both fabrics are natural and biodegradable, but both raise concerns around animal cruelty and sustainability. Large-scale cattle ranching has been associated with deforestation and biodiversity destruction, greenhouse gas emissions (methane from the cows), as well as excessive water consumption (including from leather production). In addition, leather tanning requires a lot of chemicals that expose workers at tanneries to skin and lung conditions. (Fortunately, many tanneries are phasing out these chemicals.)

On the other hand, wool emits way more greenhouse gases than, for example, cotton. An Australian wool-knit sweater emits about 27 times more greenhouse gas emissions than a cotton-knit sweater (per research by Circumfauna, an initiative of collective Fashion Justice).

With all of this in mind, how can you purchase and wear leather and wool in a sustainable way?

- Buy secondhand wool and leather products when you can. Thankfully, a lot of secondhand leather jackets and shoes are available.

- Take care of your wool and leather garments so they can last longer in your wardrobe and even be passed to other users when you donate them, for example. A lot of resources go into making these products, so do all you can to extend their life and keep them away from landfills.

- Buy recycled wool. Wool is relatively easy to recycle and some brands use recycled wool (see more on recycled wool in the preceding section).

- If you need to buy new leather or wool, consider buying from certified cruelty-free and responsible sources like the Responsible Wool Standard, for wool, and the Leather Working Group (LWG), for leather. While these certifications offer some reassurance about a product being more sustainable than its conventional counterparts, the certifications aren't perfect. For example, LWG focuses mostly on the tanning process, not the entire supply chain for leather products.

WARNING

The process for turning bamboo into fabric requires a lot of chemicals, and some of these chemicals are very toxic. There are some promising advances in processing that may mitigate this issue. Time will tell! But in the meantime, you can look out for *bamboo lyocell*. This form of bamboo requires fewer chemicals than the alternative (bamboo rayon). Bamboo lyocell is processed using a closed-loop system means that no chemicals are released into the environment.

Innovative sustainable fabrics

There are some completely new eco-friendly fabrics that are becoming increasingly popular. These fabrics are artificially made, but many mimic natural fabrics.

REMEMBER

Sustainability innovations are new, evolving, and yet to become commonplace. They are not perfect, either. Some of the plant-based leathers contain some plastic (typically bioplastics made from plant sources) but are still currently not biodegradable or only biodegradable under controlled industry conditions. However, they're a glimpse into a future where people continue to innovate as they navigate a path to a more sustainable future. Even though they are flawed, I prefer not to write them off completely just yet and plan to continue to watch the space and hope they fix some of these challenges.

If you've been looking for a vegan, sustainable leather purse, I've got you covered. Some innovative, sustainable fabrics include:

>> **Tencel:** Tencel is a versatile fabric ranging from cottony to silky. I have a tencel dress that feels like a heavier silk. Tencel can be used for denim, activewear, intimates, dresses, pants, and shirts. Tencel is essentially a more-sustainable version of viscose made from wood pulp from sustainable sources. (See Chapter 3 on environmental issues related to viscose.)

Tencel require less energy and water to produce. It is manufactured in a closed-loop system that recovers and reuses solvents, thereby minimizing the environmental impact of production. This eliminates waste from chemical solvents escaping into the environment and is also just less wasteful. Closed-loop systems reuse production waste to create new products. This is a sustainable way to preserve resources, and in the case of chemical handling, keeping chemicals from being released into the environment.

>> **Piñatex:** Imagine wearing a pineapple — okay, just kind of, as the fabric is actually made from pineapple leaves. Piñatex is a leather-like fabric. I love that it's made from a by-product of food production. Pineapple leaves that would be thrown away are made into a plant-based leather.

Although Piñatex is made from pineapple leaves, it is not 100 percent biodegradable. Its composition is 80 percent pineapple and 20 percent PLA (plastic made from corn-starch, which is only biodegradable under controlled industry conditions). Piñatex continues to grow in popularity.

>> **Apple leather:** Another new leather-like fabric that is getting more popular is made from apple peels. It's awesome to see more leather alternatives made from (mostly) plant-based materials and not *PVC* (polyvinyl chloride, a type of plastic). Apple leather is born from the Tyrol region of Italy, which is known for apple growing and processing. To combat what was otherwise significant waste, local manufacturer Frumat made a new vegan leather fabric. Veerah, a vegan shoe brand, makes stunning shoes from apple leather. To me they look like regular leather and the shoes are just as stylish. Just like Piñatex, apple leather is not 100 percent biodegradable as it has some synthetic components.

>> **Econyl:** I am a proud owner of two Econyl swimsuits. Econyl is a sustainable nylon made from recycled synthetics such as plastic, synthetic fabric, and fishing nets. It's an eco-friendlier alternative for making swimsuits. Econyl is a high-quality, Italian fiber made by Aquafil. In addition to using recycled fabrics, which is always a great choice, it also uses less water to process than virgin nylon, yet it is the same quality. Mara Hoffman, Do Good Swimwear, Elle Evans, and For the Dreamers are some examples of brands that use Econyl for swimsuits.

>> **Recycled Polyester (rPET):** This is made from recycled plastic bottles. It's eco-friendlier than virgin polyester that has to made by extracting oil. It also requires less water to make than virgin polyester.

WARNING

Econyl and rPET are more sustainable than their virgin coun-terparts but still shed microfibers. Microfibers (a type of micro-plastic) are tiny plastics that shed from synthetic fibers when you wash them, and they end up in oceans.

TIP

Wash your synthetics in a Guppyfriend bag and consider purchasing these fabrics for outfits you don't wear too often and thus won't need to wash frequently. Chapter 10 provides tips for reducing microfibers in your laundry.

All these fabrics are improved alternatives, but I'm excited to see what sustainable options become available in the future. I don't know about you, but I am curious to see and feel the purse that Stella McCartney made from mushroom leather (mycelium leather). Yes, you read that right. It's leather made from mycelium, which is the root-like system of mushrooms. Other interesting leathers you may see in stores in the near future include Cacti leather, MuSkin leather (from fungus), and leaf leather.

Understanding What's in It for You

Sustainable fashion is made at a much slower pace and on a much smaller scale than fast fashion. This has environmental benefits but also has some benefits to you as a consumer. You get durable quality clothes that are better value for your money. Consider this a bonus if you pay for choosing fashion that is better for the earth. Obviously, quality varies by brand, but I would say most sustainable brands value quality. This section goes into how sustainable fashion benefits you, the consumer.

Quality items that are designed to last

Quality garments are better for the planet. Period. Because they are built to last, they can have a life after their current owner has stopped loving them. Also, if you no longer have use for an item that's still in good condition, you probably won't just throw it away; instead, you may try to sell it, give it away responsibly, or even keep it for your kids! My daughter has asked me on several occasions for some of my clothes when she grows up, reminding me that some of my clothes will pass on to her.

REMEMBER

Quality is part of a sustainability equation. Sustainable fashion is *not* disposable fashion.

Sustainable brands take pride in their quality fabrics and craftsmanship. When you start shopping sustainable brands, trust me, you will be wowed by the quality.

I truly believe that sustainable brands produce well-made garments, to the same degree as high-end brands, at a fraction of the cost. To be clear, I'm not comparing smaller sustainable brands to Chanel. I'm talking about comparing sustainable brands to those sneaky overpriced brands whose quality does not at all match their prices.

Quality is related not only to craftsmanship but also to safety. Clothes that are free from toxic chemicals tend to be safe to wear for any age. With mass production, in contrast, maintaining quality is very challenging. For example, fast-fashion brand Shein was found to have toxic chemicals even in kids' clothes. Super scary! Sustainable brands ensure safety by sourcing fabrics from certified nontoxic sources, using toxic-free, eco-friendly dyes.

TIP

As evidence of confidence in their quality, many sustainable brands have resale pages on their websites where customers can sell their preloved items, often at a discounted price. If you aren't sure whether you love a brand, you can keep costs down by purchasing their preloved clothes items.

QUALITY ITEMS ARE MADE BY TALENTED CRAFTSPEOPLE

One way sustainable brands produce quality items is by working with excellent craftspeople — people who have generational knowledge from skills and techniques passed on from their ancestors or working with multigenerational, small family-owned businesses.

An example is New York–based slow-fashion brand Rujuta Sheth. Their signature hand-loomed fabrics are made in rural India. The fabrics are made by skilled people who have generational knowledge of the techniques. These beautiful fabrics are made without the use of electricity!

Passion Lilie, a New Orleans–based fashion brand, is well known for vibrant prints. The brand works with skilled artisans in India who design and make beautiful hand-blocked/woodblock prints. Hand blocking is a centuries-old printing technique popular in India, China, and other east Asian countries. The artisans use hand-carved teak wood blocks that are dyed and stamped by hand into fabric, resulting in beautiful prints.

Some sustainable brands work with multi-generational family-owned factories. For example, Veerah shoes works with a family-owned fair-trade factory in Taiwan, and there are many brands that work with multi-generational family-owned shoemaker factories in Italy. Some brands make garments in small design studios: for example, OffOn in Lithuania, and Thief and Bandit in Nova Scotia, Canada.

Small batches and made-to-order items

While fast-fashion brands have a lot of inventory and frequent restocks, sustainable brands work differently. Sustainable fashion is associated with less being produced and less frequent restocks. Instead, many, sustainable brands focus on small batches or sometimes made-to-order items. This isn't a bad thing! This gives the brands more time to focus on quality and better treatment of their workers. Made-to-order items can take up to six weeks to get to you. Brands with a slower fashion orientation are not focused on pumping out trends to mass market.

Many of my friends whom I have introduced to sustainable fashion express some frustration that sustainable fashion takes longer to get to them (some items are made to order so as to reduce waste) and that clothes sell out fast. And I get it; we have all gotten accustomed to clothing being available super quick from fast-fashion brands that always have something new available. You have to adjust your expectations and shopping practices a little. Here are some ways to get your hands on those slow fashion items you love:

TIP

>> **Sign up for restocking alerts or waitlists.** Many best-sellers come back year after year. Sustainable brands focus on bringing timeless, well-made apparel to the market and not high trends. If well received, the item is likely to come back.

>> **Pre-order items you know you want.** Quality fashion is worth waiting for.

>> **Check resale sites.** You may be able to get preloved items from sustainable brands immediately and much cheaper.

Timeless designs that won't go out of style

Sustainable fashion is great for unique statement outfits, but it's also excellent for quality staples that stand the test of time. Look to sustainable brands for a great pair of black pants, a white tee, or a button-down shirt, for example.

But even the unique pieces are timeless, not based on trends, but on design, beauty, and functionality. Sustainable fashion garments are typically designed to have 30 wears and a life after you. Sustainable brands are also great for forever fashion and for investment pieces.

Assessing a Brand's Feel-Good Factor

So how do you find sustainable brands? The best tip I can give you is to just start looking online. Once you are actively looking, the search engines or social media algorithms will note your preferences and start sending earth-friendly goodness your way. Once they detect a pattern, they won't even show you fast-fashion ads.

In Chapter 16, I provide a list of ten brands that are verifiably sustainable, but this list is merely a sample, not an exhaustive list. Lists and directories are out there that can aid you in finding great sustainable brands. But many times you'll find a brand on your own — not from my list or anyone else's — that checks a lot of the sustainability boxes and feels good to you. I call this the feel-good factor. The feel-good factor in this context refers to an intangible, a feeling, an impression, something about a brand that makes you feel that it places a high value on being ethical and sustainable. I'm not focused on a brand having the highest sustainability scores from organizations that rate sustainability, but rather what you are able to see for yourself from looking at a brand's website, stores, and any information available to the public.

Of course, early on in your sustainable fashion journey, as a newbie, you may not yet know what to look for, but if sustainability becomes part of your value system, you'll gain more and more confidence. Without too much outside help, you'll be able to look into a brand and make your own informed judgment about its values and whether it has a feel-good factor around sustainability. I have walked this same path, and as I've become more seasoned, it has become easier for me to make these assessments. To begin assessing a brand's feel-good factor, take note of the following:

>> **Read the brand's story and values.** The first place I check is the "about us" page of a brand's website if it has one. Even small brands tend to have websites, as they have become less expensive to obtain and maintain. Sustainable, ethical brands tend to detail their history, their commitment to sustainability, and how they achieve their sustainability goals.

REMEMBER

Sustainable brands are not perfect, and many continue to work to improve their processes. They provide certifications or information on how they are committed to quality. I have seen many sustainable brands improve over the years.

>> **Check for inspiring images or videos.** Sustainable brands take pride in their processing factories and fabrics, and feature them on their websites. Don't forget to check social media too! Look for archived live chat discussions and stories that may give you a peek into informative discussions around sustainability.

>> **Observe whether the owners/founders are visible.** Sustainable brands tend to be small, but even the bigger ones tend to have a hands-on founder. The founder's passion for sustainability is often a big part of the brand.

>> **Read about their processes.** Most sustainable brands take a lot of pride in the quality of their garments and often detail how they source fabrics, and even how they cut, weave, and dye their fabrics.

TIP

If, after reading through a brand's website, you still have lingering questions about its sustainability practices, the Good on You app is a useful resource that rates brands, both the good and the bad, on their sustainability performance.

Chapter 6

Buying Less but Choosing Well

V
ivienne Westwood was an iconic fashion designer known for creating punk fashion in the 1970s and 1980s. But throughout her momentous career, Westwood was also an activist and shared her views on capitalism, consumerism, and climate change. She believed in the need to change our spending behaviors so that we can protect the climate and people. Her advice to "buy less, choose well, and make it last" has become an iconic rallying cry for sustainable fashion. This principle should be applied to all the clothes you buy, thrifted clothes, clothes from sustainable brands, and even fast fashion.

Sustainable fashion gurus refer to this practice as *shopping intentionally* (meaning you only purchase quality, long-lasting items that you love and wear often). Why shop this way? It's better for the environment, and it's cheaper in the long run.

In this chapter I provide some guidance on how to shop intentionally, which includes evaluating the quality and durability of clothes, and deciding whether you'll be able (and willing) to wear those clothes for years to come. I also define the concept of a capsule wardrobe and help you put together your own. Many people's wardrobes are full of unworn clothes and shoes, but this chapter helps you do better than that — for yourself, and the environment.

Thinking Long Term

Shopping for trendy items takes up a lot of your time because you're always shopping for the newest style. It's also wasteful because you are wearing these clothes and shoes for a short time and then disposing of them, wasting your money and sending clothes to landfills when they go out of style. Studies show that that fast-fashion clothes are typically worn only seven times and then discarded. Statistics vary but indicate that people only wear about 25 percent to 50 percent of the clothes they buy. Intentional shopping involves thinking about the long term: for your closet, your wallet, and the planet.

When there are stores that sell inexpensive clothes, you may not worry too much about whether the item will retain its quality for a long time. If that $5 T-shirt wears out, you can just go right back to that store and buy a new item. But I expect you've become conscious about the adverse environmental impacts of the over-consumption associated with fast fashion, and you want to take a long-term approach to consuming fashion and get on a more sustainable path. To do that, you need know a bit about cost per wear.

Calculating cost per wear

This may sound strange, but the cheapest clothes you own are the ones you wear the most and for the longest time. How do I know that? Well, first of all, I'm not talking about the price you paid at the register. I'm talking about the *cost per wear* (CPW), which is the cost of an item of clothing divided by the number of times you wear it. CPW is a mathematical way to prove that clothes that are inexpensive at the register end up being more expensive in the long run.

To really change your shopping habits, you have to change your mindset. If you associate the cost of items with what you paid at the register, you have a short-term view of cost. This notion traps you into the mindset of buying cheaper clothes that are cheaply made. That means they're usually of poor quality and don't last.

So you end up going shopping again and again to buy more of these clothes, and the costs really add up. (For more on how the cost of fast fashion adds up, see Chapter 3.) But if you wear an item a lot, it becomes cheaper, giving you your money's worth many times over.

REMEMBER

You reduce the cost of your clothes the more you wear them, but that's not possible if the clothes don't have the quality to last long enough.

CPW is important because it really shows how buying sustainably not only helps to better steward the environment but also protects your precious dollars. Ultimately, bringing a long-term, CPW mindset to the purchasing of clothes enables you to be more intentional with your shopping and facilitates making better-quality purchases.

Still not sold on the power of CPW? Try this exercise: Think about the MVPs (Most Valuable Players) in your wardrobe — items that you seem to have had forever and yet don't seem to be going anywhere. Calculate their individual CPW using this equation:

$$\frac{Cost\ of\ item}{Number\ of\ times\ worn} = CPW$$

You will see that the cost is quite low even for the items you consider expensive.

I have done this exercise with my Blundstone boots, which I bought four years ago for about $200. Blundstone boots, if you're not familiar with them, were originally made for farmers in New Zealand but are now very popular for everyday wear because they are sturdy and look good. These are my go-to boots for the fall and warmer winter days. I estimate conservatively that I wear them 30 times a year, so that's about 120 times in four years.

$$\frac{\$200}{120} = \$1.67$$

So far, my boots have a CPW of $1.67 (a conservative estimate of number of wears) after four years. The soles are still intact, and they still have more wears left!

Now, also think of the least valuable players in your wardrobe and calculate their CPW. For me it's that fast-fashion dress I bought for $60. I quite regret this purchase because the item was super trendy, and I wore it maybe two or three times but not since then. So, my CPW in very simple terms was $20. Note that unlike high quality, sustainable brands, fast-fashion items lose value as soon as you buy them because these trendy items usually go out of style quickly. That means that the item's resale value is low.

REMEMBER

CPW is in no way meant to make you think that you need to buy expensive clothes; that's certainly not the point, nor is it practical given everyone operates on a different budget. The point is that inexpensive, trendy low-quality clothes are expensive in the long run, because they will go out of style quickly, so you won't wear them for long. But higher quality clothes in a timeless style are a better value because you'll wear them more often and they are made to last.

CPW aside, you should treasure and take care of the clothes you buy so that you can keep them for a long time, and they can be used by someone else when you no longer want to wear them. (For tips are caring for your clothes, check out Chapter 10.) But keeping your clothes longer is certainly easier if you purchase high-quality and durable items.

So how can you use CPW to help you become a more intentional fashion consumer? Here are some guidelines:

TIP

>> **Use CPW to audit your wardrobe.** See what kind of items work for you and then use that intel to shape future purchases.

This may be a lot of work depending on how much stuff you already have. If you have quite a lot, it may help to divide your clothes into a few categories (for example, work clothes, casual clothes, and dressy clothes) and then pick out your go-to outfits. Note them and calculate the CPW of those outfits.

>> **Use CPW to help you decide whether that outfit you want to get for a special occasion is worth the cost.** I admit that special occasion outfits are tricky items; you may never get them down to a low CPW because they are meant to be worn less frequently. In such cases you may want to consider renting an outfit. Renting can still be expensive, but it's definitely less wasteful!

Before you make the purchase, consider what you already own. Bringing the CPW into the equation before you buy that special occasion outfit may just get you to realize that maybe you don't need a new dress for every wedding you attend. Maybe you could borrow from friends or buy a versatile dress that can work for many occasions. Accessories and hairstyles can really change an outfit.

>> **Use CPW to determine whether the maintenance costs of an item are worth it.** Take into account maintenance costs as you purchase items, as the cost of such items adds to the CPW. Some clothes are dry-clean-only, which is fine for items like blazers that you don't have to wash often, but an everyday outfit that requires more frequent washing should be cheap to maintain.

>> **Decrease the CPW by reselling.** Sell items that are great quality but no longer serve you. Reselling is a way to further reduce the CPW of your quality clothes.

UNLIKE CATS, SOME CLOTHES HAVE ONLY ONE LIFE

Some fashion pieces have a slim chance of having a second life. By second life, I'm referring to use after their initial use buy their first owner. Clothes that don't have a second life are worn minimally by one person and then sent to a landfill as garbage. Items that have a slim chance of being reused have a high CPW, which makes them an unsustainable purchase.

Many fashion companies create clothes that are designed to be worn once and thrown away. This type of fashion includes inexpensive and flashy New Year's Eve outfits and other holiday-specific clothes, like Valentine's Day outfits, Christmas sweaters, and Halloween costumes. There is just no way to rehabilitate such items, so it's best to avoid them.

I remember being around Union Square in New York City at a Forever 21 store. The second floor was devoted to shiny NYE clothes and shoes. The shoes were obviously uncomfortable, the kind that no one would choose to wear for more than a few hours. I realized that most of those clothes and shoes would end up in a landfill very soon, and I was just a bit horrified.

Deciding which items deserve the investment

Some fashion items are worth the investment in both the money and the time it takes to find the right pieces. Generally, such items should be versatile so that you can wear them multiples times over years. Although these items cost more at the register, they have a low CPW because you can wear them often. That's how you get your money's worth!

REMEMBER

When you decide to spend less money or rush to purchase certain items, you end up with low-quality items that have a high CPW. You are better off in the long run if you spend top dollar for these items:

>> **Winter coats:** A quality coat will last many years, so take time to buy one that is good quality. I have worn my winter coat for six years! I bought it on sale for slightly under $300, and it's my go-to winter coat; NYC winters are cold and can mean up to two months of heavy-jacket wearing, so over six years my CPW is a decent 80 cents! My coat isn't trendy, but it still looks good and is super warm. It was made by a company that has been making coats for many years.

>> **Boots:** A good quality pair of boots — snow boots or regular boots — will last many years. An adult's feet tend to stay about the same size, and resoling shoes is not expensive. Take the time to get a good pair and simply have them resoled when the sole wears out.

>> **Jeans:** Good-quality, well-fitting jeans can get a low CPW because you wear them often. It's worth taking the time to get a pair that fits and will last.

>> **Little black dresses (LBDs):** A quality LBD is something you can wear on multiple occasions without people noticing that you are wearing the same thing. With just a simple change of shoes and accessories, you have a completely different look.

>> **Go-to blazers:** A blazer is versatile; you can use it to dress up anything from jeans to a dress. A good length for a blazer to be versatile is neither too long nor too short; it should end around your mid to lower crotch and should cover most of your butt.

>> **Everyday handbags:** An everyday handbag gets a lot of wear; you need it to be durable. Get a bag that allows for great functionality but also lasts. Stick to brands that make quality bags and shoes because they have mastered how to work with leather, canvas, or leather alternatives.

TIP

If paying top dollar is out of the question due to budget constraints, don't buy these items new. Consider thrifting instead. (Chapter 7 has all the advice you need to start thrifting.)

Taking on the 30-wears challenge

Climate activist Livia Firth started a #30wears challenge on social media in 2015. The #30wears campaign was designed to encourage consumers to abandon fast-fashion's overconsumption and throwaway culture, and replace it with a much slower, sustainable approach to fashion. Instead of buying lots of low-quality garments every few weeks, the idea is to buy a few more durable items that you can wear at least 30 times. This mindset complements the CPW method, encouraging both intentional purchases and mindful shopping.

The 30-wears challenge versus the never-ending wardrobe

The 30-wears concept may seem daunting, but that's only because you may have way too many clothes. (For some people, there aren't enough days in the year to get through half of their wardrobe.) If this sounds like you, you're likely to have clothes sitting unworn in your closet and end up continuously picking from the clothes you pull out of the closet most of the time. So if you only wear a small portion of the clothes you own, you probably only need those frequently used clothes.

With that in mind, the 30-wears challenge can be used as a shopping aide. It can inspire you to buy only the clothes you truly like or need rather than buying items just because they are on sale. This 30-wears mindset gives you confidence to be a proud outfit repeater. Outfit repeating is great for your budget and closet space, and it's also better for the environment.

You versus the marketing tactic or sale

As you shop, you may find asking yourself, "Will I wear this 30 times?" a little vague. If an item is cute enough coupled with a convincing sales associate, you may say yes when you're not really sure. A critical part of mastering the 30-wears challenge is avoiding impulse purchases. (Chapter 4 provides some guidance.)

TIP

If remembering to wear every item of clothing you own seems a little overwhelming, get some help! There are apps out there like Stylebook, Cladwell, and My Wardrobe that help you plan your outfits and track your progress with re-wearing what you have. (See Chapter 2 for more on styling apps.) Try following sustainable fashion bloggers or hashtags. Knowing there is a community out there with similar values really helps keep you motivated.

Sizing Up Quality

Sometimes it's not easy to figure out what good quality clothes and shoes should look like. Even some expensive brands can have questionable quality.

REMEMBER

Something that looks good on the hanger or display in the store and holds up after washes and wears is what you want to buy. Poor-quality clothes are more expensive in the long run.

Quality is influenced by two things: the quality of the fabric and how well-made the garment is. In simple terms, quality clothes won't fall apart after a few wears and washes and are made of fabric that feels good on your skin. You've probably had an itchy sweater. Unless you have a wool allergy like me, a good wool sweater should feel soft rather than itchy on your skin. Knowing what to look for helps you identify high-quality garments and avoid low-quality ones.

This section helps you determine if the clothes you're considering are good quality or a trap.

Feeling fabric quality

Brands that focus on sourcing quality fabrics tend to have better-quality garments, and the reverse tends to be true as well — brands that don't focus on quality fabrics tend to produce low-quality garments. Here are some tips to help you size up the quality of fabric.

Feel the fabric

Good quality fabrics tends to feel soft to the touch. Quality wool and cotton are made from long fibers. Through the spinning and weaving process, a longer fiber length results in a smoother surface with fewer exposed fiber ends. Fabrics made with long staple cotton, for example, don't pill or tear as much and can even become softer over time. Fabrics made from short fibers are not as soft because loose ends of the short fibers poke at your skin. This explains why higher quality sweaters tend to be less itchy than poor-quality ones.

Pima cotton is a higher-end type of cotton with a longer fiber than conventional cotton. It's said to be the best-quality cotton as its fibers are extra-long, resulting in soft, durable cotton. Some sustainable brands use organic Pima cotton.

Examine the fabric weave

Fabric weave is simply how thread and yarn are interwoven into fabric. A tight fabric weave results in a more durable fabric. You can easily observe this with sweaters and cotton tees. Wool that is high quality is more tightly woven, and you should not be able to see through the wool. There shouldn't be gaps either.

TECHNICAL STUFF

Wool quality depends on the source. If animals are stressed and malnourished, they don't produce good wool, so it's always better to get wool from ethical sources.

Check for signs of pilling

Pilling is small balls of fluff on a knitted garment. Wool naturally pills, but it shouldn't be excessive. Cotton from quality sources should not pill. If a cotton or wool garment is pilling in a store, don't buy it.

Hold the piece to the light

Clothes don't have to be thick to be good quality, but they shouldn't be so flimsy that you can make out objects behind the garment when you hold it up to the light. Hold a $5 T-shirt to the light and you'll probably find you can make out some shapes. This means that the fabric's weave is very loose, and that's why it won't last through more than a couple of washes. Fabric can be soft and lightweight, but it shouldn't be transparent.

Pull at the fabric

Pull at the fabric; if it doesn't retain its shape after being pulled, it's a sign that it won't last long with wear and washing. Clothes made from stretchy fabric should go back to their original shape after a pull; otherwise, they'll lose their shape easily.

Critiquing construction quality

You need to look at all the patterns and details of a garment to get a sense of the quality of work that went into making it. Look at zippers, hems, the quality of the stitching, buttons, and buttonholes. Examine the key features to make sure they are up to snuff. If most of these parts are in good condition, it's probably fair to say that you've got a great quality garment in your hands.

Zippers

Unzip and then zip zippers; there shouldn't be any resistance as you do this. Otherwise, the zipper will need replacing. Also, zippers should be neatly concealed so they don't catch the fabric of the clothes. Check to see whether the zippers match the color of the fabric; they should complement the fabric unless it's part of the design. Zipper brand YKK is well known for excellent quality, and brands that use YKK zippers tend to focus on quality.

Buttons and buttonholes

Buttonholes should be well stitched and reinforced so they don't fray easily. Buttons should fit tightly in the buttonholes and be stitched firmly with no loose threads.

Seams

Seams are the stitching line where two pieces of fabric are joined. They're what hold your clothes together, so it's important that seams are done well. Otherwise, the clothes will come loose and rip. If the seam has loose threads or uneven stitching, it's evidence of low-quality workmanship and a low-quality garment overall. Pull the seams gently apart and if it separates easily, the seam is weak and will unravel easily. Good seams should be sewn using French stitching, which looks like a single row of stitches visible from the outside, and two rows visible on the inside. French stitching is a sign of good tailoring methods and is achieved using a single-needle sewing machine.

Pockets

Good pockets are a sign of quality workmanship and general good quality. When you feel for pockets and they're not there, it means that the brand may have cut corners, but the garment should have had pockets. Pockets should be functional and deep enough to be used — to fit your phone or a small wallet, for example.

Hem

Look at the bottom of the garment and check to see if the hem is even. Check to see whether the stitches look sturdy. You don't want a hem that will come loose after a few wears.

Check for pattern alignment

For clothes with patterns, look at the shoulder seams and observe whether the pattern on the sleeves aligns with the pattern on the rest of the shirt. In poor-quality tops, they may not align. Imagine a stripped T-shirt where the stripes are slightly off between the sleeves and rest of the T-shirt. That would look a little silly, and it's a sign of careless craftsmanship.

Searching for perks

Some brands include some extra details that are further evidence of good quality and attention to detail. These details increase functionality or ensure you can repair the garment, which gives the garment a longer life. Some of my favorite features include the following:

>> **Extra buttons:** Extra buttons and matching thread are a nice touch and a sign of a quality brand that knows that your clothes will last many years and may need a button change.

>> **Adjustable straps:** Spaghetti straps should be adjustable because people have different torso lengths. Tops and dresses with adjustable straps are a sign of commitment to quality and wearability.

>> **Clear care instructions:** Washing is probably the most important part of maintenance, so washing instructions should be clear on the labels. I have seen some labels that are just not easy to understand, with lots of symbols and

crosses. I do more of my shopping at sustainable or smaller brands, and most have labels that are clear and written in words. Providing clear care instructions is a sign of a brand that is committed to clothes lasting through many washes. It's also a sign that clothes are made in small batches with better quality control, and not just mass produced.

Stay away from clothes with embellishments, feathers, and the like. Such clothes require dry-cleaning, and unless you plan to spend time and money on dry-cleaning the garment, you'll either put it in the washing machine (causing it to fall apart faster) or you won't wear it.

TIP

A lot goes into making quality garments. At first you may be overwhelmed by what to look for, but with time it almost becomes intuitive. Before you hit the racks, it may be helpful for you to look at a garment you own that you love and have kept in good condition. Observe the details. That should be a great visual of what quality should look like.

Assessing quality online

Shopping for high-quality clothes online can be a bit more challenging. You can't examine the clothes online as you can in person in a store. The images shown on websites don't show details like buttons, and you can't feel the fabric. But that doesn't mean you shouldn't shop online or that you can't find great items. (In fact, Chapter 7 shows you how to thrift online, and Chapter 13 points out some great online stores and brands.)

There are ways to figure out whether the cute clothes you find online are high-quality:

>> **Read reviews.** Some brands allow customers to review items and provide feedback on the clothes/shoes. Many of these reviews are related to fit and quality; look before you buy.

>> **Peek at the brand's social media profiles.** If you see a lot of negative comments on a brand's pages, that may be a red flag that the company has quality issues.

>> **Look at the brands "about us" page for quality cues.** Does the brand talk about fabric sourcing, quality, the

processes it uses, and the pride it takes in its quality? If so, it's likely that they strive to create high-quality items.

» **Check inventory levels.** If a brand has too much inventory and too many styles, that may be a sign that the brand focuses on mass production rather than producing quality pieces.

» **Search for lifetime warranties and repair services.** Some brands offer lifetime warranties and repair services. If they do, it is likely because they are so confident in the quality of their garments. Otherwise, they wouldn't want to be regularly called upon to repair garments they have sold.

Choosing between natural fibers and synthetic fibers

Before you start to try on clothes or put them in your virtual cart, you'll want to decide whether you prefer clothing made from natural fibers or synthetic fibers. Arguably, there are pros and cons to both options, but while I've got you here, I'll give you my two cents' worth.

From an environmental point of view, I always prefer natural fibers. They are biodegradable; not made from *petrochemicals* (chemicals derived from crude oil); and when organic, free from harmful toxins. Even from a quality perspective, organic linen is durable and has amazing natural water-wicking properties that keep you cool in the summer. Organic cotton is super soft and breathable.

Synthetics like polyester are made from oil and are essentially plastic. Synthetic fabrics shed microplastics — tiny plastics that are shed when synthetic fibers are laundered. These microplastics then pollute our rivers, oceans, and soil (more on this in Chapter 3).

WARNING

But it's important to know that from a quality perspective, there are some poor-quality natural fibers. A label that says "100 percent cotton" doesn't necessarily mean that the cotton is good quality. This cotton may be conventional cotton grown with harsh pesticides. (Chapter 3 explains the negative environmental impact of conventional cotton.) Brands that are not focused on quality may use cotton made from short fibers, which is cheaper but leads to pilling and holes. Good-quality cotton is made from long fibers (like Pima cotton).

TIP

Natural fibers are better than synthetic ones from a quality and environmental perspective. But as a sustainable fashion consumer you may want some type of reassurance that your natural fibers are ethical and sustainable. This is what you need to look out for:

>> **Fair trade natural fibers:** When a natural fiber like cotton is marked as fair trade certified, it means that workers and farmers received fair wages and that safety standards were met. Fairtrade certification also certifies that no *GMO* (genetically modified organism) seeds were used, as those require a lot of toxic pesticides. (For more about pesticides and GMOs, see Chapter 3.)

>> **Organic natural fibers:** These fibers are free from harmful pesticides and chemicals and produce safer, nontoxic products.

See Chapter 5 for more guidance on sustainable natural fabrics and fabric certifications.

Exploring Capsule Wardrobes

You surely have seen or know of people who always look effortlessly chic. Chances are these people are not spending a lot of time looking for clothes each morning, throwing their clothes all over the place. Instead, they may have a capsule wardrobe: an organized set of go-to looks that they can style interchangeably.

A *capsule wardrobe* is defined as a selection of interchangeable clothes that complement each other and that the owner loves to wear.

The purpose of capsules is to always have something suitable to wear without owning too many clothes. They allow you to put together great multiple looks without looking like you are wearing the same thing repeatedly. You maximize the clothes you own by creating multiple outfits centered around some key pieces/ staples.

THE HISTORY OF THE CAPSULE WARDROBE

Capsule wardrobes seem to be a new concept that's popular with minimalists — there are even brands that are dedicated to selling capsules — but the concept has been around for decades. *Vogue* magazine featured an article in 1941 titled "$100 Campus Wardrobe," which featured a few wardrobe essentials that a college girl could style interchangeably for versatile looks.

Flash forward to the 1970s: Susie Faux, a boutique owner in London, noticed that her customers were spending a lot of money and time buying multiple outfits that would go out of style within the season. So Faux came up with the capsule wardrobe, a collection of essential, timeless pieces that could last several years.

Donna Karan further popularized capsule wardrobes when she launched her Seven Easy Pieces collection in 1985. This collection featured seven outfits centered around a black bodysuit. Susie Faux wrote *Wardrobe: Develop Your Style & Confidence* in 1988 (published by Piatkus Books) as a guide on building a well-planned versatile wardrobe.

People who do capsules tend to be drawn to classic timeless pieces that don't go out of style and last a long time. It's a sustainable approach to consuming fashion, as it encourages a more mindful approach to shopping and a longer-term view of fashion items. Capsule wardrobes are popular today and are favored by minimalists who value owning fewer clothes, sustainable fashionistas who want to shop less for environmental reasons, and people who value the convenience of having go-to outfits. A capsule wardrobe may be just what you need to live a more sustainable lifestyle.

Capsule wardrobes can seem limiting at first glance; you may wonder how it is possible to live with so few clothes. Capsules vary in size, but the key is not to run out before laundry day. Most people wear only about 20 percent of their clothes all the time, so you probably already kind of have your own version of a capsule, just not as organized or intentional.

People oftentimes assume that capsule wardrobes lack "color," as most capsules take on a more neutral color palette. (Capsules are usually set up this way because picking neutrals, especially for foundational pieces, makes it easier to create an outfit that matches.) But a capsule wardrobe doesn't have to stick to a neutral palette. I know some people who are killing it with mixed prints and could probably come up with a colorful capsule. It is critically important for fashion to be accessible and inclusive, so I don't want you to think that you must change your style to make a capsule wardrobe. The goal is to always have something to wear, and it's a process, not a set of rules.

REMEMBER

Capsule wardrobes don't need to look the same or have a specific minimalistic style aesthetic. A capsule wardrobe does not define your style; it's your style that defines your capsule wardrobe.

You may also be thinking that you must get rid of all your stuff and have just a few clothes to go down the path of a capsule, but that's not the case. A capsule can be a subset of clothes you already own for a specific part of your life, like your work clothes. You can create multiple capsules for different occasions like travel, work, everyday wear, or different seasons.

Personally, I don't think I can create a summer capsule because I live for warm weather and varied summer looks and dresses, but I struggle with what to wear in winter. My winter wardrobe is not organized and planned well, so capsuling for winter is my goal.

TIP

If you have a lot of clothes that you probably won't be able to get to during the year, use a capsule for some sort of a rotation plan; you may just uncover some gems that have been long buried in your closet. Then the next year you can rotate new looks from your closet, which may just help you shop less!

Creating your capsules

The benefit of a capsule closet is that you always have something to wear. You may look at your closet full of clothes and still get overwhelmed choosing something to wear, which is even worse if you are in a rush. Thinking about what to wear can be frustrating and time consuming. A capsule wardrobe helps ease your frustration because you have a selection of well-planned, go-to outfits that you can pull out of your closet once your roll out of bed. Now that saves you a lot of time!

Capsule wardrobes look different for everyone. They depend on your unique lifestyle and clothing style preferences. There's no magic number for how many pieces a capsule wardrobe should have, but I've seen that 30 to 40 pieces tends to be a popular number. So, time to get "capsuling"! Here are some tips:

>> **Define your style.** A good place to start is your closet. Audit your closet to see what outfits are your go-to's. This can help you define your style based on what styles you seem to like the most. If you don't like what you have, take a look at Pinterest and create mood boards for inspiration.

>> **Do some research.** I suggest looking at capsule guides on blogs or Pinterest. No need to reinvent the wheel; a lot of blog posts and capsule templates are out there for you to refer to. Look at a couple that reflect the style you desire. While they may look different, you'll see that they tend to have similar foundational pieces. Foundational/staple pieces form the basis of your capsule; these are the things you mix and match.

>> **Create some outfits.** Go back to your closet and see what you can put together. (Sustainable fashionistas always shop their closets first!) What's missing becomes part of your intentional shopping list.

You don't have to buy *everything* that is "missing" based on what you see in these guides; instead, think of the things that are missing as items that would make your capsule more complete by providing what you need to maximize the potential of the other clothes in your capsule. For example, if all you have are bedazzled or ripped jeans, you may want to buy a pair of simple blue jeans, which will expand your styling options.

>> **Choose your color scheme for your capsule.** Your capsule wardrobe will grow with time, but creating a capsule is easier if you choose a color palette. People who capsule favor neutrals like black, white, grays, beiges, browns, and nudes because they are easy to match — but you can make a colorful capsule. The goal is to maximize the potential of your clothes, making you shop less.

TIP

If you want to make a colorful capsule, choose two or three colors that complement each other. Too many colors will be hard to mix and match. (Chapter 2 has details on color wheels.) If you want to work with prints, make sure you choose prints that are similar.

REMEMBER

You can make a capsule wardrobe on any budget; you don't have to buy high-end investment pieces. You do, however, need quality items for many wears and washes. (Take a look at the earlier section "Sizing Up Quality" for tips on purchasing high-quality pieces.)

Gathering the capsule wardrobe essentials

There are several types of garments that are considered essential for building a capsule wardrobe. These capsule essentials provide the foundation of what you need to create a variety of outfits from your capsule. They're the pieces that you mix and match and accessorize to create different looks.

Putting together a capsule wardrobe comprised of intentional pieces takes time, but you should work with what you have in the interim. Your capsule wardrobe will get more versatile and better with time.

TECHNICAL STUFF

If you live in a place where there are four seasons, it's necessary to make seasonal adjustments. But if you live in a warmer climate year-round, you can get away with one capsule with a few layering pieces for colder days and travel.

The following list identifies foundational pieces for a fall/winter capsule. Use this list as a guide when building your own capsule! I chose these pieces to suit my personal style, comfort, and weather-related needs, but as you look at other capsule wardrobe essentials online, you'll see that they have a lot in common. If the items in this list don't work for you, you can always put your own spin and color scheme on it.

>> **Outerwear**
   - Denim jacket
   - Blazer (black and/or gray plaid)
   - Classic trench coat
   - Leather moto jacket (black)

>> Tops

- Oversized button-up shirt (white; for layering and regular wear)
- T-shirts (white and black; some boxy and some for tucking in)
- Long-sleeved bodysuits (black and white)
- Denim shirt (long-sleeved)
- Cardigan (black or beige)
- Crewneck sweater (navy or black; for layering over shirts)
- Oversized sweater (black; for casual looks with jeans and leggings)
- Hoodie (gray)

>> Pants

- Denim (black plus light- and dark-washed blue)
- Straight-cut pants (black and navy)
- Ponte pants or leggings (black)

>> Skirts/Dresses

- Denim miniskirt
- Miniskirt (black or plaid)
- Slip dress (black; can be dressed up or down)
- Little black dress (LBD)

>> Shoes

- Bootie (low-heel; brown or black)
- Sneakers (white; washable)
- Flat shoes/loafers (black)
- Clogs (brown)
- Comfortable heels (black or skin-tone color)

YOU DON'T NEED TO BUILD A CAPSULE ALONE

In my opinion, the best capsules are built over time, but let's face it, not everyone has the time or patience to build a capsule wardrobe from scratch. So why not get a little help, especially since there are some options? There are sustainable brands that sell capsule wardrobe essentials!

For example, Eileen Fisher is a well-known sustainable brand. In addition to standard items, the brand offers a capsule collection (The 7-Piece Story), which includes seven pieces that you can style interchangeably to create 20 outfits. The website for this capsule is visually appealing. It features models wearing all the outfits, which helps you see the potential of the pieces.

Sustainable brand Amour Vert has a collection called Closet Essentials, which it describes as the building blocks for all-year-round outfit-repeating perfection. The collection has enough foundational pieces that you can mix and match to create multiple outfits.

Some brands might not sell capsules but offer foundational pieces that help you build your own capsule. Wayre, a sustainable travel brand, sells pieces that you can use to create to capsule wardrobe for traveling, and their pieces are easy to mix and match. Encircled, a Canadian sustainable brand, offers versatile, multifunctional, timeless pieces that could be great additions to your capsule.

For a list of other sustainable brands, check out Chapter 13.

3

Going from Thrifting Beginner to Scouting Pro

IN THIS PART . . .

Explore shopping for pre-owned clothes from thrift stores, consignment stores, and more.

Become a thrifting and vintage shopping pro.

Donate and dispose of clothes you no longer need, or those that have reached the end of their usefulness, responsibly.

Chapter **7**

Easing into Secondhand Fashion

Just as when you start anything entirely new, if you are a thrifting newbie, you may be slightly overwhelmed! Thrifting is an accessible, affordable, and sustainable way to shop. It reduces waste from clothes that otherwise would end up in landfills, and it's typically cheaper than buying new clothes. Thrifting is also rewarding, providing a lot of "OMG-you-won't-believe-what-I-thrifted!" moments. Thrifting is an excellent way for you to explore fashion and discover your sense of style at a fraction of the cost.

REMEMBER

Thrifted clothes are cheaper in general, but that doesn't mean you should treat them as disposable fashion. Thrifting should be intentional just like shopping for new clothes. If you don't think you will wear a garment much, don't buy it. No need for a pile-up in your closet. Accumulating clothes you're not wearing increases the chance that you will dispose of them in unsustainable ways. If you don't love something, leave it for someone else who sees themself wearing it more often.

In this chapter, you will find information about the ins and outs of secondhand shopping, including where to shop and how to score some great stuff. You will also find tips on how to shop for secondhand items easily and effectively.

Starting Online

Chances are you've been to a thrift store. You've probably walked into one, browsed through a few racks, and then walked out empty-handed. Shopping at a thrift store, with endless racks of closely packed clothes, is a different experience from that of conventional retail fashion stores. Many thrift stores try to organize clothes and shoes by size so you can go straight to your size section, but it can still be overwhelming.

Online thrift stores, on the other hand, provide a different experience. Because these clothes are listed online, you can sort, filter, and scroll from the comfort of your phone or computer, which is easier than sorting through racks at a thrift store. Some online thrift stores offer curated secondhand items. Think of an Etsy secondhand clothes seller or an Instagram/social media reseller. Others, such as thredUP, Depop, and Poshmark, are big online thrift stores with a wide range of styles.

To avoid feeling smothered by choices and clothes, you may want to start out online. I started my thrifting journey online by chance when searching for sustainable ways to dispose of kids' clothes. My online search led me to thredUP's website, where I found a new world of online thrifting and consigning. I found it easier to browse online at my own pace in the comfort of home, adding items to my favorites and taking time to decide whether I liked them.

TIP

If you know of a brick-and-mortar thrift store that you like, but you're a little weary of tackling the racks, find out whether they also have an online store. Many thrift stores have both physical and virtual options to satisfy all kinds of shoppers.

I attribute my thrifting success to how I started, even though it was by chance. I discovered the online thrifting option early in my journey, and I believe getting started online eased me into thrifting and helped me develop a love and appreciation of it. There are numerous online thrift stores; I highlight some in this chapter that I think are perfect for beginners.

REMEMBER

Online thrifting isn't all benefits and no challenges. Fit and feel are obvious examples of challenges when it comes to garments thrifted online because you can't try them on or feel the fabric. Some shoppers are discouraged by the not-so-generous return policies.

Getting started on the right foot

Thrifting online offers you the same conveniences as shopping online for conventional fashion, but there are some differences and challenges. Challenges may be related to figuring out the fit of the garments, limited size options, the authenticity of the items, and differences in how the items are listed/organized. The following tips can help you navigate these challenges and differences.

Know your measurements

Knowing your measurements is key to picking a garment online that is the right fit for you. Sizes vary by brand and the age of the clothes. Many online thrifting sites provide this information, but if it isn't provided by the seller, you can message them and ask. You don't want to be disappointed with a poor-fitting garment, and some thrift stores online like Poshmark don't allow returns for fit issues. See the section titled "Measuring yourself for the perfect online thrifted fit" for detailed instructions on measuring yourself.

TIP

Consider thrifting brands that you are already familiar with so that you have some idea of the fit as a start. Also, look at a garment you recently purchased that fits well and has a similar cut to what you are looking for, find the size chart, and use it as a reference point to compare with the secondhand item you are considering buying online. Another option is to start with less-structured or free-flowing garments, where getting the right measurements is not as important. Avoid final sale items.

Use sort and filter

What makes online thrifting less overwhelming than shopping in a brick-and-mortar store is the ability to sort and filter for what you want. The bigger online thrifting sites like Poshmark and thredUP allow you to sort and filter by price, brand, size, color, occasion, garment length, and more. If you know you want a knee-length, formal red dress, plug those requirements into the filter and *presto!* Now that's way easier than sifting through racks of clothes at a physical store.

WHEN SIZES AREN'T TRUE TO SIZE

Some of the garments sold online may be listed in sizes from countries that use different sizing from what you're accustomed to; for example, continental European or UK sizing is quite different from American sizing. Hopefully, the seller includes a description of whether the sizing is American, continental European, or UK, but this is another example of why asking for measurements is important when shopping online. For a brief illustration, these clothes are the same size: USA size 8 is the same as UK size 10 and EU size 38. Some clothes designed for multiple markets by international brands like And Other Stories, H&M, or Top Shop list all the sizing for the markets in which the clothes are being distributed, but a brand primarily catering to a local market may not, so be sure to look closely at the measurement information.

Find more photos

On most online thrifting websites, the garments are not shown on a model, which is what you're probably accustomed to, to help you get a visual idea of fit and style. In brick-and-mortar stores, you have the opportunity to try on the garment — not only to see if it fits, but also to see how it looks — but this isn't possible online.

What I do is google the item description and see what comes up in google images. Usually, you find that the brand has had an item listed and shown on a model. From there, you can see more details on the model's height and weight, so you can gauge length, size, fit, and possibly more details regarding color and pattern.

I was recently interested in a secondhand Helmut Lang silk blazer that I saw online but had trouble visualizing the fit, so I googled it, and voilà, images of the blazer on a model were online! If not for those other images, I wouldn't have known that the blazer was tighter and shorter than I expected. I decided not to buy it, keeping money in my pocket and leaving the blazer available for someone else.

Can't find any additional photos on your own? Don't shy away from asking the seller for more pictures of the clothing and for more details that are important to you like a close-up image of a listed flaw. Sites like Poshmark are great because the seller can load up to ten photos of the item.

Check to see whether an item is truly secondhand

WARNING

Not everything carried on resale websites is secondhand. Sometimes wholesalers also sell on these sites, which is okay, but if secondhand shopping is your goal, it defeats the purpose if you end up with new fast-fashion items.

Here are some tips to help you spot an item that is wholesale rather than secondhand:

>> The seller has multiple sizes of the same item. With secondhand, items tend to be one of a kind, unlike standard shopping where there are usually many copies of the same garment. If a seller offers multiple sizes, there is a good chance they are selling new, possibly mass-produced, fashion items.

>> They use mostly stock images. A seller that is not a wholesaler likely has photos of the clothes on a hanger taken at home.

>> The seller doesn't actually have the item in stock but purchases inventory from a third party. This is called *drop-shipping*. Thankfully, sites like Depop have banned drop-shipping because it goes against their sustainability objectives. When using the drop-shipping method, sellers find on-trend items on inexpensive websites and list them on resale apps at a significantly marked-up price. If something feels off, ask the seller questions and probe a little.

Research the brand

When I am interested in secondhand clothes from a brand that I'm not familiar with, I research the brand, as online I can't physically examine the clothes. For me, this is typically the case for the more expensive secondhand pieces, usually from higher-end brands. I do my research by looking at the brand's website to verify original price ranges and by checking out their social media profiles and hashtags, to see how regular folks like me look in their clothes and what customers say about the brand.

This may seem like too much work, but it's not; the 15–20 minutes it takes for you to find insightful information about the brand is well worth it if doing so may enable you to score a coveted item. If you feel like you're onto something, invest that little bit of time to do research.

Start out small

Rather than diving headfirst into a sea of online stores, take some baby steps. Start out shopping from just a few online stores that have stuff you like and whose platform you can easily navigate. So much merchandise is available secondhand online that checking all the platforms for items you want isn't practical; you'll probably end up getting overwhelmed and failing to choose. Just as you have specific brands you typically shop from, stick with a small number of online thrifting stores, especially at the beginning of your thrifting journey.

TIP

Once you find online sellers/resellers that you like or that have a selection of items that appeal to you, follow them on social media. They typically have more photos and possibly some styling videos, and you can easily DM them for more details. This can make your search for future purchases much easier.

Give fast-fashion items a second life too!

I can be a thrift snob and tend to shy away from fast-fashion items in thrift stores. Fast fashion is mass-produced, inexpensive, and trendy fashion. Examples of fast fashion include clothes from brands such as Zara, H&M, Shein, and Fashion Nova. (For more on fast fashion, see Chapter 3.)

But the truth is there's a lot of fast fashion out there and you shouldn't have to avoid it, especially if you like the items. The goal of thrifting is to find amazing clothes and keep them in circulation and out of landfills for as long as possible. Since you are giving a fast-fashion item a second life, you are still shopping more sustainably than if you bought the same item straight from the factory. If it's thrifted, it's a win!

Beware of scams

Sadly, we live in a world (and perhaps always will) with scams. There are scammers in online reselling! Watch out for red flags like the seller asking you to pay them directly, not within the reselling app or site or asking that you communicate through their personal email. Depop provides buyer protection for up to 180 days for scams and will give you a full refund if you purchase on the app.

Going down the rabbit hole of online thrift stores

A ton of online thrift options are available for all budgets and styles, from your local Facebook Marketplace group to curated online vintage stores to goodwill.com. Here's a quick roundup of the best online thrift sites, especially if you're just getting started with online thrifting:

>> **thredUP:** thredUP is probably the biggest player in the online thrift space in the United States and Canada. This online consignment store sells merchandise sent to it via its cleanout kits by folks like you and me, as well as clothes it receives as a resale service partner for big brands such as Rent the Runway, Adidas, Fabletics, Crocs, and so on. My first online thrifting experience was on thredUP.

The website is user-friendly and allows you to filter by size, brand, category, occasion, and lots more. thredUP has a variety of clothes, shoes, and accessories from high-end designers to everyday affordable fashion for women and children. They also allow you to return items that don't work out for you for a small restocking fee. thredUP also has a points and rewards system that includes benefits like waiving restocking fees for some purchases.

>> **Poshmark:** Poshmark is a social peer-to-peer e-commerce app where sellers in the United States, Canada, and Australia can sell their clothing, shoes, and accessories. A lot of stuff from popular brands end up on Poshmark. You can even buy specialty clothing items like wedding gowns on the app. I have sold some items on Poshmark. Unlike thredUP, which handles all logistics, on Poshmark it's done by the seller, but you will receive notifications from Poshmark.

Poshmark allows you to filter by brand, size, shipping fee, and condition. Expect higher prices but also great deals! Plus, you can negotiate prices. Poshmark does not allow for returns unless there are serious flaws with the item, so be sure to ask for measurements or more details if you aren't familiar with a brand.

>> **The RealReal:** Yes, there is an app in addition to brick-and-mortar stores you are probably more familiar with. The RealReal is a high-end consignment store. All the merchandise has been authenticated so there are no fakes. If you are looking for a vintage item or designer-brand luxury items, the RealReal has a lot of options.

The RealReal lets you filter by size, price, occasion, color, and so on for men, women, and kids. The store is U.S.-based but offers worldwide shipping.

>> **Vestiaire collective:** Vestiaire is a global luxury resale platform with a community of sellers and buyers from around the globe. Just like The RealReal, it has authenticated luxury and designer brands. You can filter by brand, category, vintage, shipping options, and more.

>> **eBay:** eBay is a multinational e-commerce site for both peer-to -peer and business to consumer sales. Chances are you have been on eBay at some point. eBay has a lot of stuff, so it can be overwhelming. Lots of people have experience with the site and can offer advice on how to navigate it. If shopping for secondhand fashion is your goal on eBay, filter by auction to avoid wholesale businesses that may be selling new fast fashion. Also, be aware that there are scams on eBay (see the earlier section "Beware of scams" for how to avoid them).

>> **Depop:** Depop, like Poshmark, is a peer-to-peer social e-commerce company. It's known for unique items in addition to other regular items for women and men. The app is available in the United States, the United Kingdom, Australia, New Zealand, and Italy. Depop has upcycled and handmade items in addition to secondhand merchandise. When you set up your account on the app, you select your style preferences and size. Your home page will include suggestions based on your preferences. You can also search for specific items.

Measuring yourself for the perfect online thrifted fit

TIP

One thing that will set you up for online thrifting success is to know your measurements. Sizes vary by brand, and vintage sizes can be different. Try to focus on measurements and not numerical sizes. Doing so saves you money, the hassle of returns, and costs of alteration; plus clothes look best when they fit you right, so take the tape and measure yourself.

Here's what you will need:

>> **A flexible measuring tape:** This can be found easily at most superstores and fabric stores and should be included in most sewing kits.

TIP

If you don't have a measuring tape, you can use a string or ribbon and measure that against a ruler.

>> **The right bra:** Wear the bra you typically wear or the one you plan to wear under the garment you are measuring for.

>> **Close-fitting clothes or just undergarments:** It's harder to measure accurately in bulky clothes you; you need the tape to be as close to your skin as possible.

>> **A mirror:** Looking at yourself in the mirror helps you maintain the correct posture and keep the tape straight.

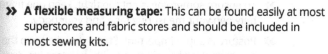
TIP

Alternatively, for harder-to-reach areas, you can ask a friend or family member for help.

Getting comfortable with measuring yourself

Measuring is a pretty basic skill, but when you're measuring for fit, you want to do it correctly. So follow these basic steps to measure yourself:

1. **Hold the 0 end of the tape measure in your dominant hand so the numbers are facing away from your body.**

   If you're not good at reading upside down, turn the tape measure so you can read the numbers.

2. **With the other end of the tape measure in your other hand, move your hands to what you want to measure.**

   You may have to circle your body or stretch straight across your shoulders or down your arm.

3. **Write down the measurement (and maybe the date, if you're someone who likes to keep track of those things).**

TIP

As you measure, keep these tips in mind:

>> A good time to measure yourself is after a meal. You want to be able to breathe in your new outfit after eating.

>> To ensure something is not too tight, keep one finger between your measuring tape and your body.

>> Posture is super important. Stand straight, keep the tape measure straight, and stand with your legs hip-distance apart.

TIP

If you find it hard to measure yourself, or if you're just not confident in your measurements, find a local tailor or seamstress and ask if they'll take your measurements. Note the date you had the measurements taken and have yourself re-measured periodically. Many dry cleaners have a tailor available on certain days. The prices vary, but I have paid $10 for the service before. I live in New York City where everything is more expensive, so you may be able to get this done for less.

Keep reading for instructions on measuring different parts of your body. Refer to Figure 7-1 to see exactly where on the body to place the tape measure.

Measuring your bust

You need to measure the fullest part of the bust. You want to make sure the garment fits the fullest part of your bust. Wrap your measuring tape around your back and across the fullest part of your bust. The number where the two ends of the measuring tape meet is your bust measurement. Make sure the tape is straight across your back and your bust. This can be challenging to accomplish on your own, so use your mirror.

Measuring your waist

You need to measure the narrowest part of your torso, usually right below the ribs. It's higher than where you think your waist is. Another way to find the spot is to bend your body to either side. the indentation (or crease) is your natural waist.

REMEMBER

Some garments have different types of waists; for example, drop waists and low-rise jeans are below your natural waist.

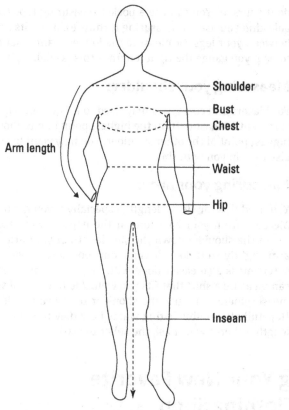

FIGURE 7-1: Measuring different parts of the body.

Measuring your hips

To measure your hips, you need to measure the widest part of your hips—not the hip bone. Identify the widest part of your hips and then wrap your measuring tape from the back of this position to the front. The number where the two ends of the measuring tape meet is your measurement.

Measuring your inseam

If you are purchasing pants or shorts, you'll need to know your inseam measurement. To find this measurement, measure from the top of your inner thigh down the length of your entire leg (for pants) or thigh (for shorts). This is a measurement that is probably much easier taken with the help of someone else, but you can do it yourself. You can use a pocket measuring tape (the retract-able kind you use for measuring furniture), using its case as a grip between your legs. Or measure the longest pants that fit you best to help you gauge the right length if this is challenging for you.

Measuring your shoulders

For blazers and coats, you may need to know your shoulder measurements. Measure from the highest point of one shoulder to the highest point of the other shoulder. You may want to ask someone else to help you with this.

Measuring your arms

You need this for sleeve length, especially if you are tall or petite. Measure from your backbone at the nape of your neck over the top of the shoulder down the side length of your arm. Bend your arm slightly so it doesn't come out too short on you. This measurement is also easier done with help, so as an alternative you can measure a shirt that fits you well. You might find some online measurements that use the shoulder to sleeve for sleeve length. Hopefully the online listing states how they measured the sleeve length; otherwise just ask the seller to clarify.

Finding Your New Favorite Used-Clothing Shop

There are many different places you can shop secondhand. You're probably more familiar with charity stores but there are also chain resale stores and consignment stores. Charity thrift stores are not-for-profit, while chain resale stores and consignment stores are for-profit businesses.

The for-profit/not-for-profit distinction doesn't necessarily matter. Both options are more sustainable ways to shop and keep clothes out of landfills and in circulation longer. If you are looking to support charitable causes by shopping secondhand, then make sure to look out for this distinction as you plan your thrift store trips.

TIP

You can easily locate the closest thrift stores to you through Google, Yelp, or any other search method you use. But there are a few blogs and resources dedicated to thrifting that provide information on thrift stores. I stumbled upon a national thrift store directory at thethriftshopper.com, a website that lists thrift store locations by zip code and even has some reviews. I liked the website because it expanded the radius I could consider for my thrifting store patronage and opened a world of thrift stores that I didn't know.

Ultimately, finding your favorite thrift store depends on you and what works for you. It may be convenience, experiences at the store, or finding the gems you desire in a store. The thrift store that was my favorite at the beginning of my journey was conveniently located, so I attribute the choice of that store early on to its convenience. It was located close to my favorite spa, my primary care physician, and my kid's orthodontist. It was a small store but was great for me. It was in a fairly wealthy neighborhood, with great, lightly used clothes. My best blazer and vintage coat are from that store. I made it a habit to see what they had on the days I was over there.

TIP

When you find a store that you like, go often. As you get to know the people who work in the store and build a relationship, you may get information on upcoming sales and when new stuff is coming to the racks.

Doing good by shopping at charity stores

When you think of thrifting, charity stores are probably what come to mind. You are likely familiar with Goodwill and the Oxfam shops in the United Kingdom. A charity store is typically run by a nonprofit that sells donated goods to support charitable projects and organizations.

Charity stores tend to have a fair amount of inventory because of the sheer volume of donations. Many people have dropped off donations at their local charity store at some point. For more information on donating responsibly, go to Chapter 9.

The bigger charity stores have multiple retail and outlet store locations across the country. Chances are a charity store retail or outlet location is close to you. The retail stores are the first stop for donations, and after items have been on the shelf for a while, they are sent to the outlet stores and sold by the pound. I have never been to an outlet, but if you have an eye for fashion, time, and patience, you can bag yourself some great deals. This may be less likely for a beginner but is certainly possible for a reseller or more experienced thrifter.

Examples of charity thrift stores in the United States include the following:

>> Goodwill

>> Salvation Army

>> The Society of Vincent de Paul

>> Housing Works

Considering chain resale shops and consignment stores

Chain resale shops and consignment stores are the typical for-profit secondhand stores. From a customer perspective, chain resale stores are similar to charity stores, with similar store layout and merchandise. Consignment stores tend to be smaller and sell higher-end or designer brands.

Chain resale stores

Chain resale stores tend to have the same look and feel as charity stores, with the only difference being that chain resale stores are for-profit businesses.

This includes stores like Savers and Buffalo Exchange. Resale chain stores pay for the clothes dropped off to them. If you visit these stores, you'll notice people dropping off clothes and either receiving store credit or cash.

Examples of chain resale shops in the United States include

>> Savers

>> America's Thrift Store

>> Buffalo Exchange

>> Red, White and Blue Thrift Store

Consignment stores

Consignment stores sell clothes and shoes on behalf of the owner, who receives a percentage of the selling price. If you are looking to buy designer labels or higher-end brands secondhand, consignment stores are your best bet because people that own this type of stuff tend to want to recoup a little of what they spent. At consignment stores, clothes are vetted for flaws and authenticity, so they tend to be pricier than chain resale and charity stores. Most consignment stores are small businesses, but some have multiple locations like The RealReal or Fashionphile. Both stores resell authenticated luxury brands.

thredUP also offers consignment options through its clean-out kit. The clothes and shoes don't have to be high-end or designer to consign with thredUP, but they are selective regarding quality and only accept clothing made by certain brands.

Preparing for Your First Thrift Store Visit

Thrift stores have a lot of great stuff, but the stores aren't organized the same way as regular retail stores. The ambiance is completely different, with no fancy lighting, enticing music, and displays — at least not at your typical thrift store. You will be faced with rows of racks and bins with clothes and accessories. It may not look fancy, but many people have found gems in mint condition even in those bins.

You can't rush thrifting; it requires patience and an open mind. Thrifting is overwhelming, especially if you don't have a plan for what you are looking for. At the beginning of my journey, I left stores within a few minutes, often empty-handed.

TIP

Thrift lists can come in handy. A thrift list is simply a wish list of items you want to thrift. (See Chapter 15 for a sample thrift list.) But it's totally fine if you don't have a thrift list quite yet; you can still go and browse, and you could get lucky! I once got myself a beautiful, brand-new Cynthia Rowley dress with a $475 price tag for $45, a reward for my taking a chance by walking into a thrift store!

This section provides the tools and strategies you need for a successful day of thrifting. Know when to go, what to do, and what to bring so you can walk out of the store with top-notch items.

Deciding when to go

While thrifting success is typically by chance (and patience), some days can offer a higher probability of success. Success here is being less overwhelmed or scoring great stuff. Here are some ideas on when to go:

» **Quieter days:** Consider weekday mornings, especially if you are new to thrifting. Saturdays are super busy, and you may get overwhelmed.

» **Beginning of the week:** Consider the beginning of the week because most thrift stores restock on Mondays as most people drop off donations over the weekend.

» **During spring cleaning season:** Traditionally, people do their spring cleaning between the months of April and May, so donations tend to spike around that time.

» **After long holidays:** A few people declutter and clean up over long weekends. A lot of this stuff is donated to thrift stores.

» **Thrift store sales days:** Just like regular stores, thrift stores have sales days. On these days you get additional discounts. Many discount days are not known in advance, but if you happen to be around a store location that has a sale day, go into the store, as you could just get that special item on your list at a steal.

WARNING

Avoid well-publicized sales days like Buffalo Exchange's $1 sale. These sales tend to be super crowded, so they may not be the best for a beginner.

WARNING

Don't go thrifting when you are tired or hungry. You need some patience and focus. If you are hangry, you won't have the stamina to sort through stuff and could miss out.

Navigating the store

Just like every store, stuff is organized by category, color, and sometimes by size. Depending on the size of the thrift store, shoes may have their own section or be displayed above the shorter clothing racks. Here are some tips as you navigate the thrift store for the first time.

» **Have an item and section in mind.** If you are looking for a specific item, like women's shoes, go to that section first and see what they have. You're likely to be more successful in thrifting if you are focused and not randomly searching through endless racks of clothes.

>> **Pay attention to items at the end of racks, around the dressing rooms, and even at the checkout counter.** These are items that sparked some other person's interest, and although that other person didn't end up buying them, they may be good items.

>> **Hold onto items that catch your eye.** Don't rush to try on one item but keep it in-hand and keep browsing. Don't get too excited to try on one item that might not even fit and miss on out other great stuff. Thrift store items are typically one of a kind.

I've had a leather jacket on my thrift list for a while but missed out on one because I didn't use this strategy. I was at a consignment store and got distracted by a pair of strappy Celine heels. The lady at the counter even offered to hold them for me while I shopped, but I was overeager. While I was busy trying on the shoes, another lady walked in and picked up the leather jacket of my dreams. She purchased the jacket, and the heels didn't fit me.

>> **Stand back and take it all in.** I do this when shopping sales racks in conventional retail; I take a step back and look at the rack from a distance. Because clothes are tightly packed together, standing back can give you a better view.

REMEMBER

Bring your etiquette to the store. You may be excited to get first dibs, but the polite thing to do is to follow behind the shopper who's ahead of you. Don't come at them from the opposite direction.

Dressing for thrifting success

Many thrift stores have limited fitting rooms. Thrift stores need to maximize square footage, so they don't have a lot of changing rooms. The lines can be long, and you want to be courteous to other shoppers, so think of wearing clothes that are easy to slip off and on. Don't wear a complex outfit with several layers if you expect to be using the fitting room. Also, in the event you can't get to the changing room, wear clothes that are easy to put other clothes over. Aim to be hands-free — not all thrift stores provide carts, so use a hands-free cross body bag to keep your hands free to carry your merchandise. It's also easier to sort through the racks and bins when you don't have to hold on to your bag.

TIP

Here's a thrift store shopping outfit idea for you to consider:

>> Fitted leggings or shorts

>> Button-down shirt with a tank top underneath

>> Small cross-body bag

>> Comfortable shoes that are easy to slip off

Examining an item before you commit to it

Because thrift items are mostly used, and even items that are new/not previously used may have some flaws, so it's important to examine them carefully. Thrift stores' refund policies are stricter than regular stores, so if you buy it, be prepared to keep it and part with the cash for good.

Here are some typical questions to consider to help you decide whether an item is worth thrifting:

>> **Do you really like the item?** Don't get it just because it's a name brand at a bargain price. You have to ask yourself whether you really like it. I am guilty of thrift snobbery or bias toward higher-end brands. I have bought some items because they were higher-end brands but ended up not wearing them.

>> **Is it damaged?** Examine items for stains, rips, and pilling. For shirts, for example, look around the armpit area for sweat marks because those are hard to remove. Examine sweaters for excessive pilling. Check pants and skirts for functional zippers. Hold the garment to light if you can, to examine for stretching and wear. Some items have repairable issues, so they are worth your time and money. Other items, not so much. (For more on how to repair clothes, see Chapter 11.)

>> **Is the item difficult or costly to clean?** If the item is dry-clean only, consider whether the cost of dry-cleaning is worth it for you. Some items, regardless of cost, can only be dry-cleaned, such as suits, blazers, and coats, but you may not be willing to dry clean a $5 thrifted blouse.

Chapter **8**

Upscaling Your Thrifting Efforts

Thrifting is one of the most sustainable ways to shop. It keeps clothes out of landfills and extends the lifespan of clothes in the hands of new owners. Thrifting has undeniable environmental benefits, so by shopping secondhand you're doing your part toward preserving the health of our environment (in addition to benefitting personally). You get great stuff for less, much less!

Chapter 7 is an intro to thrifting, providing information on where and when to go thrifting and some good practices for thrifting success, including what to wear when you're shopping and how to navigate a thrift store. Sometimes you'll leave a thrift store empty-handed. But you can also head home with some amazing, unique pieces for an affordable price. Thrifting is often considered a skill, and you can improve skills.

In this chapter, I take you beyond the beginner steps and toward pro-thrifter status. In this chapter, I give you the scoop on how to score great finds at thrift stores, including shoes and accessories. You don't need a magnifying glass, but I clue you in on how to sharpen your detective skills to find a true vintage gem. If you want to get the most bang for your buck and find outfits that make you feel special, put these tips and tactics into practice.

Finding Hidden Gems

Hopefully you thrift or plan to thrift for several good reasons, which may include a desire to help save the environment by lengthening the lifespan of clothes, supporting charities, saving money, or finding gems at a fraction of the regular price. In this section, I focus on how to find gems, because of all the reasons to thrift, scoring a unique item in great condition is probably way up there. So here's the scoop:

>> **Analyze the competition.** Who's your competition? The other shoppers, of course! A great way to spot gems is to see what other shoppers are looking at. A good place to find this stuff is around the dressing room or at the counter. Also, if another shopper looks at a garment for a long time but then puts it back, they may be on to something special that just didn't make the cut for them but may be right for you.

>> **Look at everything.** You won't find a gem within a few minutes of entering the store or by looking at a few racks. The patient thrift shopper wins.

>> **Consider a fixer-upper.** Don't let a missing button or loose hem make you lose out on a great piece. You may be on to a diamond in the rough.

>> **Keep an open mind.** If it looks remotely interesting, put it in your shopping basket and try it on. You may be surprised. It may look even better once you try it on. This is something I need to work on. I tend to have a tunnel focus at thrift stores and have probably missed interesting pieces that would add some variety to my closet.

>> **Location matters, sometimes.** Stuff from all walks of life ends up in thrift stores, but sometimes location matters. Thrift and consignment shops in wealthier neighborhoods may have more to offer in terms of quality pieces; they may be pricier but still have good deals, especially in terms of quality and brands. I have thrifted a brand-new Talbots blazer with tags on it for $30, and Talbot blazers retail for about $150.

>> **Know the winning seasons.** Spring cleaning season offers a lot more opportunities to find gems. Some thrift stores have spring sales. The lines can be long, but there are plenty of gems to go around. I have been to one and thrifted a Moschino resort outfit, new with tags for $20.

>> **Go early and often.** Finding gems is easier if you hit the stores early before they get crowded. Stores tend to get crowded around lunchtime. Go early — get there shortly after opening.

>> **Recognize quality when you see it.** If you don't know what quality looks like, you can't spot it. This may sound obvious, but it's important. Chapter 6 has more detail on spotting quality items.

One of the ways I evaluate whether an item is of good quality is by checking for pockets. It may sound strange, but it's something my mom taught me as a child; she always said that quality dresses have pockets. I have spoken with people who sew, and they have confirmed that pockets require a higher degree of skill and also take time to do right.

REMEMBER

Check the online bidding/auction sites of charity stores. Goodwill has a bidding site where some higher-end unique items are sold. Prices are still less than retail, so it may be worth a peek.

Make a date out of a thrift store visit. Go thrifting with a friend so you can cover more ground and find more gems.

TIP

Check online resale sites like Poshmark, The RealReal, and thredUP if you are looking for something specific. These sites allow you to use keywords and have a search button; for example, if you're looking for yellow clogs, type it in and see what comes up. (Chapter 7 includes advice for navigating online stores.)

Buying Used Shoes

Thrifting shoes can be challenging, and it's understandable if you have some reservations about purchasing other people's old shoes — likely concerns about hygiene. I get it. When we think of used shoes, dirty old sneakers usually come to mind. However, many thrift stores do a great job sorting out the bad apples. You may still come across some questionable footwear in your thrifting journey, but don't let this dissuade you. There may be a gem right next to those worn sneakers, and this gem comes at a fraction of the cost!

In this section I provide information on how to spot and where to find good used shoes. I also clue you in on how to clean your preloved footwear — which can be a game-changer!

TIP

Thrift stores are not the only place to buy used shoes. If you're not quite ready to thrift shoes, consignment stores and Poshmark tend to have like-new or new shoes. Consignment stores tend to be more selective in what they sell, so they may carry better-quality options. Poshmark and eBay sellers may have recently purchased items that did not quite work out for them but are either outside of the return window or are just not returnable; such purchasers may just want to make some of their money back rather than donate the shoes. These options may be pricier but still cheaper than full price.

Examining used shoes

Most people probably have an idea as to whether the shoes they're considering thrifting are in good shape. But here are a few pointers to help you decide whether a pair of used shoes is worth your money:

» Look out for big tears on the upper part of the shoes because they can't be fixed.

» Make sure the shoes have not lost their shape, as this indicates that the shoes are worn out and won't last long.

» Check to see whether the sole is firm to the touch. If it is, it still has some wear left. On the other hand, if it's soft and dark, it will need replacing soon.

» For heels, make sure the heel cap (the rubber that meets the ground) is still intact.

Knowing where to go

The thrift store is the most obvious place to go, but you can also buy used shoes in consignment stores and online on eBay, Poshmark, and other resale sites. The thrift store tends to be the cheapest option while consignment stores tend to be more expensive. Where you go depends on what you are looking for.

For example, I would consider a consignment store if I wanted a lightly used designer pair of shoes (not to suggest that you can't get lucky and pick up a near-perfect pair of shoes at your local

Goodwill store, but your chances are higher at a high-end consignment store like The RealReal). I would go to Poshmark for like-new or new conventional name brands like Converse, Vans, Adidas, and so on. I sold a pair of like-new Vans for $10, and they sold quite fast.

REMEMBER

It's helpful to know the cost of typical repairs when you are shopping for used shoes. I got a pair of gold vintage Ferragamo heels for $40 on The RealReal. The heels needed new rubber, but the cost and uniqueness of the item made it worth the cost of repair. It's a function of the cost of repair and the value of the item to you.

Disinfecting and cleaning shoes

I prefer to clean the inside of my used shoes. I use a regular rubbing alcohol on a piece of cloth and wipe down the inside of the shoes. You can also use antibacterial sprays to do so. You can also use a shoe deodorizer or sprinkle a little baking soda on the inside of the shoes to remove odors. If the shoes have removal insoles, take them out and wash them with detergent and warm water, and use a hard -bristled brush to give them a scrub.

Some sneakers — but not all — can be washed in washing machines. If they're made from nylon, polyester, or cotton, they can be machine-washed. On the other hand, sneakers made from rubber or suede, for example, have to be hand-washed; you can use an old toothbrush and a white vinegar and baking soda mix to bring some shine to your thrifted sneakers.

For thrifted shoes, disinfect the inside of the shoes and follow care instructions for the specific fabrics of the shoes. Thrifted leather shoes may need to be conditioned to remove the dirt and grime that have accumulated, and of course, you want to polish the shoes for some shine. (Find out more about shoe care in Chapter 12.)

Sorting Through Accessories

Most fashion thrifting is probably focused on clothes. Thrifting accessories may be overlooked. But thrifting accessories is a good place to start for beginners because it's less overwhelming and the sections are smaller. Accessories are typically one-size-fits-all, so your chances of finding something you like that fits are high. All the main accessory categories can be found at the thrift store. Here are a few tips for sorting through accessories.

Jewelry

Jewelry is typically displayed near the front of a store, with finer items being in glass cases by the register.

Auctions are great places to find preloved jewelry. Many thrift stores have online auctions, and many great pieces end up there. A lot of the good stuff that is donated to the thrift store ends up at the auction. Some thrift stores display the online auction items in the store, but you can also ask the store attendants or simply check online. The bids start at reasonable prices so you may get lucky. You can also find jewelry online (not on auction).

As you sort through jewelry, these pointers may be useful:

>> **Take your time and look slowly.** Thrifting is not something to be rushed, and for jewelry, you probably want to pay closer attention to detail.

>> **Inspect for flaws.** While thrift stores tend to do a good job weeding out broken pieces, it doesn't hurt to check. Check to make sure the clasps are working and look for missing stones and discoloration.

>> **Look for quality stamps/markers.** Most of the jewelry you see will be costume jewelry, but there's some fine jewelry to be found as well. Fine jewelry will have quality markers. These markers indicate the quality of metal used:

TECHNICAL STUFF

- 417, 585, or 750 indicates the gold content (10K, 14K and 24K).
- 900, 900PT, 950, or 950PT indicates the platinum content.
- 925 indicates that the item is sterling silver.
- GP means gold plated.

The markers are small, so you may need your reading glasses. If the pieces don't have these markers, you can't be sure that they're pure gold, silver, or platinum.

Another marker you may see on a piece is the manufacturer's log or the maker's mark. Most times, it's an initial or letter, but sometimes it's a short, identifiable word. If you see one, look it up. You may have found a gem.

REMEMBER

You may want to clean your thrifted jewelry because of the close skin contact it had with the previous owners, and you may need to clean off the grime and bacteria. With the exception of pearls, acrylic jewelry, and plastic jewelry, most jewelry can be cleaned with rubbing alcohol. Pearls and acrylic or plastic jewelry can be cleaned with mild, gentle soap and water. Metals and precious stones can be cleaned using rubbing alcohol.

Scarves

At a thrift store, scarves are usually tossed into a box, so they can be overlooked. The fancy high-end scarves are likely to be on display near the register or online, but you can find gems in boxes too; you just need to sort through them. Examine them for rips, pilling, and stains, and note the fabric and fabric care instructions. And just try to have fun; because scarves tend to be inexpensive at thrift stores, you can buy one or two crazy-looking ones without feeling guilty.

TIP

Pay attention to small details. Some designers may sign their names on scarves. It can be fun to find a unique piece.

Handbags

Handbags are typically easy to find at thrift stores. Thrift stores are great places to find special occasion bags and clutches. They tend to be lightly used, and you can score one at a low price. The high-end pieces are typically close to the register in display cases or hanging up behind the register.

Here are some pointers to help you sort through bags:

>> **Check for quality.** Examine the leather, zippers, and clasps. Check the quality of the stitching.

>> **Examine wear and tear.** Bags that are used every day get some significant wear and tear. Does the bag still have more wear left for you? Check the seams, straps, and zippers for signs of wear.

>> **Consider bags without designer labels.** Not every gem is designer: You may be focused on finding that Gucci bag for $6, but in all seriousness, this is rare because thrift stores sort these items and send them for auction. Don't overlook a real gem in your pursuit of Gucci. Pay attention to small details and look for a quality piece among the many unique quality pieces that may not be from a brand you recognize. Check for unique embroidery; some may even have the maker's signature.

WARNING

Clean thrifted bags thoroughly. Bags make many journeys with all manner of things in them. Use a vacuum wand or lint roller to clean up any crumbs, lint, or loose dust. Then wipe the inside with rubbing alcohol (on a cloth) or antibacterial wipes. If the bag is leather, condition the leather to protect the leather from cracks and give it a good start with you (more on conditioning leather in Chapter 12).

Belts

I have friends who swear that thrift stores are the best places for belts. Full disclosure, I am not a belts person, but it could be that I am looking in the wrong places — regular stores which tend to have boring basics that don't inspire me much. But thrift stores often have unique ones.

>> **Be bold and creative.** Belts at thrift stores tend to be inexpensive and are a fun way to collect statement accessories.

>> **Look in both the women's and men's sections.** Belts are often unisex, so if it fits and is in good condition, take it!

>> **Check for quality.** Examine the leather and make sure the hardware like the buckle still works.

>> **Try them on.** Belts are super easy to try on, so make sure you do.

HOT FOR THE GEMS BUT NOT THE SMELL

Thrifting and vintage shopping offer some treasures, but these gems might come with the signature musty thrift store smell. Some people are more sensitive to it than others. I get it! Not to get too technical on you, but this odor is from a combination of molecules from the environment and body oils that are trapped in the clothes. These odors might not be completely eliminated after your first wash, but don't stress or be grossed out. There're ways to get rid of that smell!

One method for deodorizing pre-owned clothes is to use vodka. All you need to do is put some undiluted vodka in a spray bottle and spray your clothes lightly. When the vodka evaporates, it takes the odors with it. You can follow the same process using white vinegar. Another method is to hang your clothes outside and let the fresh air and sunlight do the job for you. Once the clothes are cleaned, you can really enjoy the spoils of your thrift store treasure hunt!

Shopping for Vintage Clothes

Vintage clothes are clothes that are at least 20 years old. I dabble in vintage clothes and accessories shopping, in part because I consider having vintage items as owning a piece of history. Call me whimsical, but I always entertain fantastical notions of who may have owned the pieces and how they ended up with me. Vintage also offers a chance to have unique items that no one else has, and vintage pieces tend to be good conversation starters. I always like to proudly declare "It's vintage" after I receive a compliment.

Vintage items, in my experience, tend to be of better quality, because stuff back then was made to last. I have a 25-year-old vintage Ralph Lauren shirt that is in remarkable shape and still has many years of wear left.

Your first forays into vintage shopping can be intimidating at first, and you may get frustrated not finding that special piece, but there is something fun about that hunt.

NO LONGER A VINTAGE VIRGIN

For my first vintage purchase, I got clip-on earrings that were about as old as me! I found them on Esty (an online retailer specializing in vintage and handmade pieces). Thankfully, the seller knew the brand name. So, I set out googling and found a *New York Times* piece about the brand, Kirks Folly, from 1980 and a *Vogue* cover from the early 1980s featuring pieces similar to the one I got. Such things are interesting to me, and I like to think I have pieces of the past and they are only going to get older.

TECHNICAL STUFF Some vintage sellers are knowledgeable about the history of the brands or items and can offer interesting conversations.

How to tell whether something is truly vintage

Verifying the vintage of an item may take a little detective work. Thankfully, there is a wealth of information from vintage enthusiasts to guide you along the way. Plus, it's fun when you read about the history of a brand that may not exist anymore or how styles and detail have evolved over time as you're digging. But a lot of vintage-inspired clothing is out there, so you need some guidance on how to sort through and determine whether you are getting the real deal. You need look for some cues in such things as labels, style aesthetics, and detail/finishing.

Check the label

Labels are probably the best place for you to get information on whether something is truly vintage. Labels contain a lot of information, so if you score a vintage piece with a label, you may be able to sniff out the decade or even the year the garment was made. Look for the following info:

>> **Copyright year:** While this isn't always available, you may get lucky and see the word "copyright" and the year: for example, copyright 1980. This may be the year that the garment was made. Sometimes, though, the copyright year is related to the year the brand or logo was incorporated or trademarked, but that's easy to verify by googling the brand.

>> **Union labels:** Some vintage clothing may have union labels. The union label represents the union of garment workers that made the clothes. For some added context, to help you date vintage clothes, union labels apparently were initially proposed in the 1930s as part of the Congressional bills that, to implement public welfare reforms, focused on fair working conditions and fair pay for workers during the Great Depression. You can find these labels on clothes from around the 1930s until the late 1970s, when more and more clothes started being produced overseas.

A popular label you can find in the United States is the International Ladies Garment Worker Union (ILGWU). Some vintage enthusiasts can track this label to determine the decade the clothes were made, because the logo changed eight times. Other union labels you may see are the Amalgamated Clothing Workers of America (ACWA) or the Consumers Protection label. The ACWA (established in 1914) was a union of garment workers in the United States. By the 1920s, it was the predominant union for workers manufacturing men's clothes. Clothes with the AWCA label will predate 1976, which was when the union merged with other unions. The Consumer Labels will be on garments made in the 1930s through the late 50s.

>> **Lot or style numbers:** Vintage clothing may have a label that includes a lot or style number. This was used when more and more clothes were mass-produced in the United States but before computerization. Lot or style numbers were used as a way for factories to track garments they had manufactured. Lot numbers stopped being used in the late '70s or early '80s, probably as computerization picked up.

>> **Made in a country that no longer exists:** If the label indicates the item was made in a country that no longer exists or notes a colonial name, you have found a true vintage piece. Some old clothes made in Hong Kong may have British Crown Colony Hong Kong on their labels. Evening gowns/dresses that were made in the British Crown Colony of Hong Kong were popular in the 1960s, and this label was a mark of quality and excellent beading work. If you find an evening outfit with this label, it's probably from the 1960s. An online search shows that some of these pieces are available on eBay, Esty, and Poshmark.

- **>> Brand logos and labels that look different from the current ones:** These are easy to verify if they're from a popular brand such as Ralph Lauren, which has changed its logo over the years. If you google the info, you can find a bunch and may even be able to find the decade that it is from.

- **>> Made in the USA:** Before offshoring garment manufacturing overseas, most clothes were produced locally. Garment manufacturing shifted overseas in the 1970s, mostly to Asia. There are, of course, clothes made in the USA right now, but clothes that look a little dated and sport "made in the USA" can be vintage. Also, you can tell they're vintage if they're from bigger brands that no longer manufacture in the United States. For example, you can find vintage GAP "made in the USA" clothing on resale sites and eBay. All GAP clothes are now made overseas.

TIP

You can check a vintage label database. A few online resources and some social media accounts are dedicated to tracking vintage labels. You may get lucky and find the label of a vintage piece. The Vintage Fashion Guild at vintagefashionguild.org/label-resource/ is an excellent resource for vintage labels.

Look at the details

The label is probably the easiest place to determine if the clothes you have found are vintage, but some clothes won't have a label. If the clothes look vintage, you can look at small details like zippers and maybe evidence of hand sewing. Look for the following:

- **>> Zippers:** The difference is metal versus plastic zippers. You'll find metal zippers on clothes from the 1940s and 1950s. Before that, buttons were mostly used as fasteners for garments. Around the mid-'60s, nylon coil (plastic) was introduced.

TIP

    If you want to get a good visual of metal zippers, check Etsy, as there are sellers who sell vintage metal zippers.

- **>> Pinked seams:** A pinked seam isn't a pink color but is a method use to secure edges of the fabric, so it doesn't fray or unravel. The pinked seam looks like teeth or zig-zag edges; pinking shears were used to prevent fraying because sergers or sewing machines that can do the multiple stitches needed to finish a seam weren't available. Up to the 1960s, a good number of people still made their own clothes at home, so those clothes didn't have a label, but they did have pinked seams. If you see this kind of seam on a garment, there's a good chance it's vintage.

>> **Buttons made from early forms of plastic:** Up to the 1940s, buttons were made from early forms of plastic like Bakelite and celluloid. Plastic buttons as we know them today became more popular from the 1950s onward.

TECHNICAL
STUFF

Celluloid is an early form of plastic developed in late 1800s. It was made to look like ivory. Celluloid buttons were popular from the early 1900s through the early 1920s. *Bakelite* is another early form of plastic and is recognizable today for having an apple juice or yellow color as a result of oxidization over the decades. Bakelite was popular from the 1920s to the 1940s.

Know vintage style silhouettes

You probably have some exposure to vintage silhouettes from movies and old photos. These are often good visual cues that your clothes are vintage. The '80s styles are recognizable by their big shoulder pads, slouchy blouses, and bright colors. The '70s were known for polyester shirts with prints or long maxi dresses with deep v-necklines. The '60s sported psychedelic shift dresses.

WARNING

A lot of "vintage-inspired" clothing is on the market that's not vintage but looks like the real deal. If your goal is to buy real vintage, look out for the imposters. Unfortunately, I have bought what I thought were '90s vintage sunglasses that turned out to be vintage inspired. But I have since learned that vintage items are typically one of a kind, and if more than one piece of the same item is on sale, it's likely not true vintage.

Where to find vintage clothing

There are lots of places you can find vintage clothing, from your local thrift store to specialized stores. And don't forget grandma's closet! Vintage shopping isn't easy — it can be hit or miss — but scoring some amazing vintage pieces is well worth the effort. Vintage finds can tend to be chance finds, but your chances improve depending on where you look.

TIP

Keep vintage shopping fun! Don't be stressed out if you don't find what you want immediately. Go vintage shopping when you have time and are relaxed. Vintage pieces are nice to have but shouldn't be a necessity. So take a breath; if your vintage gem is meant to be, it will find its way to you. The following sections note the best places to find vintage items.

Flea markets

Flea markets (open-air markets for secondhand articles and antiques) are great places to score some vintage pieces, but they can be overwhelming, especially the big ones like the Rose Bowl in California. Navigating a flea market can be challenging because of the crowds, but you can really score some great vintage pieces. Take your time; make it a social day and go with a friend.

TIP

Flea markets are outdoors with no changing rooms, so wear something that you can easily wear things over. Follow the guidelines in Chapter 7.

Thrift stores

Probably the most obvious place to find vintage pieces and a really good place to look is at a thrift store. Check out the preceding section for tips on how to tell whether something is vintage. It's getting harder to find vintage clothes at thrift stores because vintage is extremely popular and thrift stores are flooded with fast-fashion donations. But you can still score amazing vintage finds at thrift stores.

REMEMBER

Vintage sizing is not the same as sizing today. Be sure to check in other size sections. A 1960s size 12 is now size 6 or 8. Your vintage gem may be hiding in another section.

Many thrift stores also have websites. Goodwill and other thrift stores have online bidding websites, and a lot of the good stuff ends up on these sites.

Vintage shops

I've found some vintage garments and accessories at dedicated vintage stores. Yes, they tend to be more expensive, but they source and make it easier to find pieces, verify pieces, and curate items but at a premium cost. The convenience may be well worth it, plus the stores are run by experts who know vintage. They can tell you about the designer and the decade the piece is from, and some even do some mending and cleaning for you. Prices vary by location. Obviously, a vintage store in New York City has higher rent, so prices there will be higher than places outside the city.

TIP

If you are on a road trip through some small towns, ask locals about vintage stores. You may score some great vintage pieces at a lower cost.

Vintage shows

Vintage shows are typically planned events where multiple sellers come together to sell vintage pieces. These events have entrance fees and higher prices but have the best stuff, so attending may be well worth the price for a unique vintage item. The Manhattan Vintage Show is an example; it's held three times a year in New York City. The Pickwick Vintage Show in Los Angeles is another example. Check for some near you!

Estate sales

If you are open to the idea, you can find vintage clothing and accessories at estate sales. Estate sales are different from garage sales; while garage sales are for selling unwanted items, estate sales are for selling everything in a house. You go to the house and browse as if you were in a store. The thought of it can seem intimidating and may not be the first stop for a vintage shopping beginner but it's good to know that they are options. You can find information online; most estate sales are listed on estate-dedicated websites.

Online

I get most of my vintage pieces online because that's where I shop for almost everything, including thrift and vintage. Examples of places you find vintage online are eBay, Etsy, Depop, The Real-Real, and Instagram vintage stores.

Here are some tips to help you navigate buying vintage online:

>> **Buy from trusted online sellers.** If you are buying on Etsy or eBay, check sellers' feedback reviews before you buy.

>> **Ask for images and ask questions about the condition of the item.** Most vintage sales are final. Vintage is old, and although it may not be in stellar condition, that's part of the character of items (imagine a well-worn vintage leather jacket). Nevertheless, still ask for more pictures so you know what you are getting. Also ask about odors.

>> **Go by measurements and not size labels.** Vintage clothing is smaller than what is listed on the size tag. The fashion industry keeps changing its sizing and labeling.

TIP

For help wading through all the online options, check out Chapter 7.

IN THIS CHAPTER

» Finding a new home for your preloved clothes

» Donating clothes to benefit people in need

» Reselling the garments that no longer serve you

» Figuring out what to do with undergarments and socks

» Sending worn-out clothes to the recycling bin

Chapter **9**

Donating, Selling, and Disposing of Clothes

Even if you are a super sustainable shopper, you'll likely decide to get rid of some clothes sooner or later. Of course, you can purchase high-quality clothes that last longer (Chapter 6), and even mend or upcycle your clothes once they start to wear out (Chapter 11). But eventually, that much-loved sweatshirt may be worn down to paper-thin and need to go, or maybe you've just decided that jean shorts aren't for you anymore. Maybe your body has changed, and you just don't want that zebra-striped bodycon dress staring at you any longer. (Been there!) So what do you do? Just throw it all in the trash?

It is estimated that a whopping 85 percent of clothes end up in landfills. But you don't want to be part of the problem. You're interested in finding ways to dispose of clothes as sustainably as possible. Don't worry; you have plenty of options.

In this chapter, I share some ideas on what you can do with your old clothes or those you no longer need. I also share tips on how to donate or sell your clothes in a way that gives them a real shot at a second life with a new owner. Finally, I guide you on how to dispose of clothes that are no longer useful for human use in an eco-friendly way (that is, not throwing them in the trash).

Giving Your Clothes a Second Life

Your first experience giving clothes a second life probably would have been during childhood if you received hand-me-downs. You may not have liked it, but that was likely your earliest experience with sustainable fashion. As the fourth of six kids, I was often dressed in hand-me-downs. If you have lived my experience, where your elder siblings' clothes were handed down to you, and for that reason, you missed out on new clothes, you probably found it to be annoying or maybe even frustrating. But as an adult, I've discovered that this kind of lifestyle isn't just financially responsible and practical, it's also super sustainable.

A lot of clothes that we no longer want for ourselves may still have some wears left in them and can be worn by others. Moreover, your items that are no longer fit for use, like your raggedy T-shirt, can be recycled into something else or even repurposed at home. If you want to avoid throwing clothes in the trash, you are not alone! And there is a lot you can do to that end.

Fashion is a form of self-expression, so chances are your old garments, which seem dated to you today because you have evolved from when you bought them, would be loved by someone else out there. You shouldn't send them off to landfills without attempting to find someone else who can make use of them. This also applies to those Halloween costumes or New Year's Eve outfits you've bought over the years.

REMEMBER

To reduce the amount of clothes you have to dispose of, take good care of your clothes so they don't wear out prematurely. Invest in quality items that can hold up over the years and don't buy more than you can (or actually need to) wear.

In the following sections, I provide some helpful guidance on how you can donate and dispose of your clothes responsibly.

Donating Clothes to Support Charitable Organizations

If you've ever bought clothes from a thrift store or heard about organizations like the Salvation Army or Goodwill, you know where donated clothes end up. (If you haven't been to a thrift store and want to know what they're all about, check out Chapter 7.) When you enter a thrift store aiming to buy something, you're the shopper, but when you donate your clothes, you're the supplier.

Donating has a feel-good factor to it: You're doing your part for charity, decluttering your closets, and keeping clothes out of landfills. Eventually, you stop loving even your favorite clothes, and if they are still in usable condition, you want to find someone else to love them.

Lots of people out there are ready and willing to love your lightly worn clothes. Thrifting is insanely popular right now as more and more people are becoming sustainably minded. In fact, some people purchase clothes exclusively from thrift stores.

The difference between for-profit and nonprofit shops

Not all thrift stores are charity organizations (see Chapter 7 for more on the difference between charity thrift stores and for-profit thrift stores). When you take your clothes to charity thrift stores like Goodwill or Salvation Army, you are making a charitable contribution. The proceeds from selling your clothes support charities in your community, and you receive a receipt that you can use to claim a tax deduction on your personal income tax return (more on tax deductions in the next section).

For-profit thrift stores like Buffalo Exchange and Crossroads Trading will buy your old clothes from you for cash or store credit. Because you sell (rather than donate) to for-profit thrift stores, you may not claim a tax deduction for the value of clothes sold to such thrift stores.

REMEMBER

You can also sell your clothes at consignment stores. Consignment stores sell your clothes on your behalf in exchange for a fee (see more on consigning clothes later in this chapter).

BETTER QUALITY CLOTHES MAKE BETTER DONATIONS

Why are vintage clothes still holding up well even decades after they entered circulation? Because before fast fashion exploded in recent decades, people were more intentional shoppers (buying with longevity in mind) and clothes were generally better quality. Fast fashion has had a noticeable impact on the volume and quality of thrift store merchandise. Fast fashion creates a lot of wasteful purchases that end up in thrift stores, or worse, in landfills. Brands like Fashion Nova have an ultra-fast-fashion business model, dropping about 600 new designs a week. That's a lot of clothes in a very short time. Because we are consuming five times more clothes now than we did in 1980, it's been reported that the amount of clothes that charities and thrift stores receive has doubled over the past 15 years, but a lot of the clothes are fast fashion and generally lower quality than charities and thrift stores traditionally received.

So, what can you do about this? Be a more mindful shopper, buy less, and buy better quality. Quality thrift starts with quality clothes. Donate the quality you would want to thrift yourself. This starts with buying quality clothes.

If you own fast-fashion clothes, take care of them so they last longer for you. Try not to buy them going forward. Of course, you can still donate the ones you have now if you have no intention of wearing them again.

The scoop on tax deductions

In the United States, Uncle Sam has been kind enough to provide you with a cash benefit when you donate to charity. Congress passed a law many years ago to encourage charitable giving, so the Internal Revenue Code (United States income tax law) allows you to claim a tax deduction on your income tax return for the value of property donated to charity.

A tax deduction reduces the amount of income on which you pay tax. This benefit comes by way of reducing the income on which you pay taxes by the value of the items you donate. But to get this benefit, you must obtain a gift receipt from the charity to which you are donating your clothes, unless the value of the donation is less than $250.

For example, if you donate to Goodwill of NY/NJ, the receipt you receive will specify the number of bags donated each of clothing, accessories, household goods, or miscellaneous, but it's up to the person donating to determine the value of the donations that can be claimed as a tax deduction. Receipts issued by charities in other places may provide more detailed itemization: for example, the number pants, dresses, coats, and so forth. You just need to be able to demonstrate to the Internal Revenue Service, in the event your tax return is audited, that your donations had the claimed value.

TECHNICAL STUFF

Single filers who earn at least $12,950 of income in a calendar year are required to file a tax return with the Internal Revenue Service by April 15 of the following calendar year.

REMEMBER

Keep the receipts you receive from the charities to which you donate for three years. This is a requirement of the tax law, as the Internal Revenue Service can ask you to produce those receipts at any time during that three-year period if your tax return gets audited.

Where to put all those clothes

Now that you know what to do with your clothes, you may still have some lingering questions about where to put those donations. I've got you covered:

>> **In-store drop-offs:** The most common way to get your clothes to thrift stores is to physically drop them off at the thrift store or at an attended donation center.

>> **Donation bins:** Some charity stores may have donation bins in locations near you. You can locate these by going to their website and searching for donation bins by zip code. These bins will have the name of the charity displayed clearly.

These bins aren't textile recycling bins (discussed in the later section "Saying Goodbye to Clothes That Have Lived Out Their Usefulness").

WARNING

You won't get a receipt (for tax purposes — see the preceding section) from drop bins.

>> **Donation drives:** Look out for donation drives in your local community. Local communities, schools, or churches may organize donation drives for charity stores.

>> **Pick-up services:** Some charity stores may offer pick-up options, including picking up directly from your house. You may have better luck with smaller community-based charity stores than bigger ones, as you can imagine Goodwill probably receives a lot of requests.

The Dos and Don'ts of Donating Clothing

Thrift stores receive a lot of unsellable clothing that sadly ends up in landfills, which ironically is what you hope to avoid when you donate clothing in the first place. Thrift stores also incur costs to dispose of these items. For example, Goodwill incurs millions of dollars annually in disposal fees, reducing funds directed to the charity projects you hope to support with your donations. Donating more responsibly can go a long way in reducing this burden on the stores.

REMEMBER

The purpose of these dos and don'ts is not to discourage your donations to Goodwill, the Salvation Army, and other charity stores that rely on your donations to support worthy programs for our communities; instead, it's to give you tips on thrift donation etiquette. Ultimately, in addition to supporting noble charitable causes, extending the lifespan of your clothes through responsible donations is positive for the environment. But it's important to do so responsibly. If you follow these tips, your donated garments have a good shot at having a second life:

>> **Don't donate completely worn-out clothing.** Don't wait for your clothes to be worn out or stained and then donate them. They won't be sold and will end up in landfills. Repurpose torn clothes into cleaning rags, for example, instead of sending them to thrift stores.

>> **Do wash the clothing before donating it.** Thrift stores don't have the resources to clean the merchandise they receive. They're operating on very tight budgets, with no resources available for washing/cleaning the clothes they receive. Dirty clothes are trashed for hygienic reasons and end up in landfills. Throw them in the wash before you donate them!

>> **Do tie your shoes together when you donate them.** Shoe pairs can easily get separated during the sorting process at donation centers, so be sure to tie them together — no one

can buy one shoe! Goodwill requests that you keep shoes as a pair — tie laces together or put a rubber band around them so they don't become separated.

» **Do check for flaws.** Items with fewer flaws are more likely to be sold. Check the clothes you plan to donate for holes and small tears, and if you can repair them, please do! (Chapter 11 tells you how to make some commonly needed repairs.) If you are not inspired to do small repairs on items you plan to donate and the items are otherwise in good condition — especially if they are from a well-known brand — donate them anyway. A savvy thrifter may buy the item and repair or upcycle it.

» **Don't just dump your donations at the door of a thrift store.** Donations should be handed over to a thrift store representative. Drop off donations to your local thrift store during working hours and wait until they are properly received and accepted by an employee. If you leave items at the doors of thrift stores without the items being properly accepted, the stores can't accept them. They consider such items as potentially contaminated and usually just throw them away. Moreover, properly handing off your items to employees of thrift stores is not only a courteous thing to do but is also the only way to get your tax donation receipt! (Read the earlier section "The scoop on tax deductions" for more info.)

WARNING

Improperly dumping your donations at the doors of thrift stores is illegal in some places, putting you in peril of prosecution and fines.

GIVING THROUGH BUY-NOTHING GROUPS

If the prospect of trying to sell your clothes sounds tedious for you or if you are looking for another way to offload your clothes in a way that supports your community, consider "buy-nothing" groups.

Buy-nothing groups are local gift groups where people in a local community (typically a neighborhood) come together to give away things

(continued)

(continued)

for free. Buy-nothing groups were conceptualized by The Buy Nothing Project, founded in 2013 to encourage giving things with no money exchanges within the community. This is done by creating local gifting communities, primarily organized through Facebook groups. It's a great way to offload your unwanted items quickly yet still do good for your local community. Plus, you can get your stuff off your hands in a few days or even a matter of hours.

Someone will probably take your warm coat, lightly worn winter boots, and lots more. If you are a parent looking for ideas on what to do with lightly worn kids' clothes (kids practically outgrow their clothes overnight), perhaps check your local buy-nothing group and gift a neighbor as a way to let go of them sustainably.

Making Some Cash by Selling Your Clothes

You don't always have to donate or give away your preloved clothes for free. Instead, you can make some money while doing some good by selling your old clothes!

REMEMBER

Donating clothes is a generous act that helps people in your community. But there is no shame in trying to earn back a bit of the money you spent on your clothes! You are still doing something good for the world because you're prolonging the lifespan of your clothing, rather than adding to massive landfill piles. You can feel good about guaranteeing that they have a new owner.

There are a few ways to sell your old clothes. You can make money by consigning your clothes; selling them yourself on reselling apps like Poshmark, Facebook marketplace, or Depop; or selling them to for-profit thrift stores.

Consigning your clothes

Consigning your clothes simply means that a third party is selling your clothes on your behalf for a fee. This third party is what is known as a consignment store.

When you consign your clothes, the store selling your clothes takes a commission. The commission varies, but it's typically 30 percent or 40 percent (a 70/30 or 60/40 split).

While 40 percent may seem high to you, it takes the headache away from listing the clothes yourself. Plus, the clothes are taken from you right away, so you get to declutter as you wait for the sale. The store does the marketing and display for you. Consignment stores typically have loyal customers who come to the stores looking for what you are selling, mostly preloved high-end or designer brands.

TECHNICAL STUFF

Most consignment stores are small local businesses, but there are also bigger consignment stores like The RealReal, Fashionphile, and Vestiaire Collective.

Here are some things to keep in mind when consigning your clothes:

>> **Consign your higher-end fashion.** Consignment is better for well-known, higher-end brands as this is what consignment shoppers are typically looking for.

>> **Note the season.** If your clothes are in season, they are more likely to sell.

>> **Consider the location and vibe of the consignment store.** Brands do differently in different locations. If the store is in an upscale neighborhood, traditional designer clothes will typically do well there. If it's an online consignment store, check out the store's social media to see what they sell and what sells fast.

Don't take it personally if the store rejects your clothes or shoes. They're not being snobbish; they're simply small businesses that have a bottom line to consider. They know the business well and what will sell to their customers.

Don't give up because of one rejection. Another store in a different neighborhood or with a different vibe may be interested.

>> **Inspect your garments thoroughly for any major flaws.** Flawed items are hard to sell. If a pair of shoes has a faulty strap, for example, a customer trying it on will notice and the consignment store will send it back to you, so don't waste your time or the consignment store's time.

>> **Be okay with the prospect of your stuff being discounted.** Remember the goal of consigning is not to recoup your costs but to make money from your preloved items.

REMEMBER

While consignment stores take a big cut, they are likely your best bet for your high-end designer items. Customers trust that stores have authenticated what they sell. Stores like The RealReal ensure that customers are getting true preloved designer items.

If you don't have any luck with your local consignment shops, consider thredUP, an online thrift and consignment store. While most consignment stores sell mostly high-end or designer items, thredUP consigns clothes at all levels from fast fashion to designer items. thredUP is selective because they receive a lot of stuff to sell, but if your items are in good condition, there is a high chance they will be accepted. Items not accepted can be sent back to you or donated. The payout isn't very high, but it's super easy to send your clothes to them using their clean-out kit, which you can order on their website for free.

Selling clothes to secondhand stores for cash or credit

Some for-profit secondhand/thrift stores will buy your clothes from you. You typically have an option to receive cash or a trade credit. Here are some tips for selling your clothes to secondhand/thrift stores:

>> **Find out which brands or styles the stores want.** It's best to ask the stores beforehand what they are looking to buy. Some bigger stores may have trend reports on their website with more details on what they are looking for that season. These stores can be picky, but they are just running a business!

>> **Choose the days you drop off your clothes wisely.** Some stores have a mail-in option, but many times you will be going into the store. Lines can be long, so try and go on less busy days. Find out ahead of time if they only buy on specific days or at certain times.

>> **Be courteous and patient.** Secondhand/thrift stores know what they are doing. They are retail experts and know their pricing. If their pricing doesn't work for you, move on and don't argue.

>> **Ask whether they offer consignment.** For some higher value brands, secondhand/thrift stores may offer consignment, which may result in a higher payout. Typically, these are items that are on display behind the checkout counter in the stores.

REMEMBER

If your clothes are from a sustainable brand, check and see whether they have a secondhand marketplace where customers can sell lightly worn clothes from the brand (see more on secondhand marketplaces in Chapter 5). If you are looking for an additional perk of shopping from sustainable brands, this may be one of them. It's a convenient way to give your clothes a new home while also making a little money.

Selling your preloved clothes by yourself

You probably have a lot of stuff that won't make the cut for consignment stores, but that doesn't mean that you can't make some money by selling them yourself. When you sell clothes yourself, you cut out the consignment middleman. But that doesn't mean you need to go door-to-door or shout in the village square like a medieval peddler.

There are plenty of apps and websites that help you sell your clothes, shoes, and accessories online, all by yourself. Some of the popular platforms include Poshmark, Depop, eBay, and even Facebook Marketplace. While consignment stores do the posting and display of items for you, on these reselling platforms you post the items online yourself, set prices, and ship the items. These platforms still take a commission from your sales because you are using their platforms, but you're the one making the decisions and doing the heavy lifting. It may sound daunting, but it's totally doable!

Here's what you can do to improve the chances of your stuff selling on reselling platforms:

>> **Have patience.** Reselling on these platforms can be a long game. Don't rush to delete your listing after a few weeks — it may still sell. But if you want to declutter quickly, this may not be the best option for you.

>> **Use clear images.** Make sure the pictures give a true representation of what the item looks like. Take pictures in good lighting against a solid background. Take detailed shots of the garment or shoes up close. You can take pictures of yourself in the item so prospective buyers can picture themselves in the outfit (you don't have to show your face; you can take a picture from the neck down).

>> **Create an effective, descriptive title.** Make sure you have a good descriptive title and text so that prospective buyers know what you are selling and your listing is searchable. Poshmark best practices suggest a title that clearly states the style, brand, and fabric, using searchable keywords. For example, Stella McCartney (brand) high-waisted black (style) linen pants (fabric), US Size 8 (size). In this way, your listing can come up on a Google search or on the app you're selling on. If the item has special features like "limited edition" or "new with tags," add that to the title.

>> **Write a thorough description.** In addition to a descriptive title, include a clear description of the item. This reduces back-and-forth questions from prospective buyers, which can be time-consuming and annoying, especially when they don't end up buying the item. Useful things to include are the condition of the item; measurements if you have them; and any sellable features like deep pockets, soft fabric, or comfort, which can help a prospective buyer make a quick decision.

>> **Set a fair price or low starting bid.** You don't have to sell at giveaway prices, but you shouldn't overprice either. Pricing can be arbitrary on these apps, and there is really no formula, but if you want to sell quickly, a lower price will get you there. Check the apps to see what other resellers are selling similar stuff for. Make sure you understand fees/commissions, if any, and how discounted shipping will impact the price you set (shipping is typically on the buyer, but free or discounted shipping can help sweeten the offer to the buyer). Leave some room for negotiation with a buyer in your price.

Saying Goodbye to Clothes That Have Lived Out Their Usefulness

At some point, your clothes are going to be worn out and need to be discarded. But luckily for you, there is a growing textile recycling industry fueled by concerns for the environment. Improvement in the technology has been driven by the volume of clothes that we just can't keep pushing into landfills. These options are becoming much more accessible, meaning you can feel less guilty when you have no choice but to throw your old clothes away.

You may have seen clothing recycling bins in a variety of public locations like parks, gas stations, and parking garages.

Some fashion brands may take some of your worn-out clothes for recycling! Sustainable brand For Days is one such example. For Days has a great recycling program called the Take Back bag (fordays.com/products/take-back-bag). The Take Back bag costs $20, but in exchange, you receive a $20 credit toward purchases from them. They will recycle your worn-out clothes from any brand, but what they do with their own clothes is even better. For Days is working hard on becoming a zero-waste circular fashion brand. Circular fashion involves using and circulating clothes responsibly and effectively in society for as long as possible, only disposing of them when they are no longer fit for use. For Days achieves this by designing all their clothes to be 100 percent recyclable — they make them into new yarn to make new clothes.

Although more options are now available for recycling your clothes, don't get rid of your clothes prematurely. The 15 percent discounts some fashion stores offer when you put your old clothes in their recycling bins is obviously very appealing. But the not-so-great side of these bins is that many of the clothes deposited at popular fast-fashion stores still have some wears in them. The store may not sort through the items put in their bins, like For Days does, to salvage clothes that can still be reused.

REMEMBER

Most textile recycling is what is known as downcycling. *Downcycling* is the recycling of waste where the recycled material is of lower quality and functionality than the original material. An example is when your old clothes are made into carpet padding or insulation, which is commendable, but downcycling garments that still have wears left in them is not what you want to be doing. Sending clothes to a recycling bin should be your last resort, and only done when clothes are beyond use and repair. Throwing clothes in the trash shouldn't even be on your list anymore!

TIP

While you can easily send your old clothes to those recycling bins, consider repurposing some of these old clothes for cleaning rags or even DIY projects. Extend their life in your home a little longer before you throw them away.

Dealing with Undergarments and Socks Sustainably

There are some items that you may feel awkward about donating. They're usually also items that shouldn't be used by another person for hygienic reasons. Those kinds of items are bras, underpants, and socks.

Most people have never thought of their bras, socks, or underwear as things that people can wear secondhand. These items are tricky because we all have lots of them and need to dispose of them at some point. The following sections include some ideas about what you can do instead of throwing your old undergarments and socks in the trash.

Donating bras

While most thrift stores don't accept bras, there are other organizations that will accept your bra donations, so you don't have to throw your bras away. You have three options: Donate lightly used ones to charity, send them to brands that accept used bras for recycling, or donate them to local textile recycling programs.

Some examples of charities that accept bra donations include the Bra Recyclers (www.brarecycling.com/recycling-form) and Free the Girls (www.freethegirls.org). Free the Girls is a charity organization that takes clean, gently used bra donations to human trafficking survivors in Mozambique, Costa Rica, and El Salvador. The Bra Recyclers donates bras to nonprofit organizations around the world. To participate in their program, all you need to do is wash your bra and fill out the online recycling form.

Some undergarment brands like Knicky recycle underwear and bras. Go to `knickey.com/pages/recycle` for how-to details.

Don't forget to check lingerie brands at your local mall. Some may offer bra and underwear recycling bins.

TIP

Getting rid of old underwear

You likely won't be able to donate your undies, but you probably don't want to throw your old ones in the trash either, if you can find a more eco-friendly alternative. Some alternatives are available for you to recycle your underwear. Your options are underwear recycling programs offered by brands or textile recycling bins.

>> **Parade:** A sustainable underwear brand, Parade, has partnered with TerraCycle, a recycling company that specializes in hard-to-recycle materials, to create a national recycling program for underwear. You can order the recycling bag for free on their website (`www.yourparade.com/products/second-life-recycling-kit`). You can recycle any underwear brand with Parade and get 30 percent off your next purchase with them.

>> **Knickey:** This lingerie brand recycles bras, underwear, socks, and tights and repurposes them into insulation and mattress padding. You receive a 15 percent discount.

>> **Textile recycling bins:** You can also recycle using your local textile recycling bins. You can find these bins through a Google search (add your location to find options close to you). Just double-check what they accept before you drop off your undies.

Recycling and repurposing old socks

When you notice a hole (or three) in your socks, you may think the only logical place for that sock to go is in the trash. But there are other options. And there's no need to throw out all your partnerless socks in a rage. Try repurposing unwearable socks by using them as cleaning rags. You can use them to wipe whiteboards or to make ice packs or dog toys. A sock also makes for a good cleaning mitten.

As with other textiles, socks can be recycled. After carrying around old socks for years, I literally had a small basket full of my kids' baby socks. I shipped them off to the Smartwool recycling program, a brand that sells socks. I was sent a bag in the mail, and I just shipped it back after filling it with my old socks (www.smartwool.com/shop/second-cut-project-take-back-mail-in-bag). Zkano, a family-owned sustainable sock brand, recycles socks (zkano.com/pages/zkano-recycles). Sustainable underwear brand Knickey also recycles socks in addition to underwear and bras.

If you have socks that are in usable condition, but you've lost their pair, you don't have to get rid of them. Another option is to wear them mismatched! I doubt that many people really care whether your socks match. What matters is that your feet are warm.

4

Keeping Your Clothes and Shoes in Tip-Top Condition

Take care of your clothes to keep them in your closet longer.

Explore basic sewing, mending, and upcycling so a little wear and tear doesn't mean sending clothes to a landfill.

Extend the life of your shoes.

Chapter **10**

Caring for Your Clothes

O nce you buy something, the most sustainable thing you can do is take care of it so it lasts. It saves you money and means that less stuff needlessly ends up in landfills. Knowing that you are doing your best to keep your clothes in good shape is a good feeling. I always like to think that even if you tire of your clothes, the next owner should get them in the best possible shape. Yes, wear and tear happen, but excessive wear and tear can be prevented with good care.

I have picked up a lot of tips over the years on how to look after my clothes, and I share them with you in this chapter. Not sure what items should be handwashed and which should be dry-cleaned? Do you usually give up on a shirt once it gets a stain? This chapter tackles all those questions and more, like how to properly store clothes and care for specific types of fabric. How you do your laundry and how you store your clothes really matters. Treat the clothes in your closet with care and devotion, and you'll be doing your wallet and the earth a favor.

Doing Laundry with Clothing Longevity in Mind

When you think about wear and tear, you probably think of the damage that happens as a result of wearing your clothes, like rips and tears, but your clothes take quite a beating in the washer and dryer. Clothes are not supposed to last forever, but they shouldn't be ruined after a few washes either. Granted, there are too many poor-quality clothes out there that won't last in any case, but laundry habits and machine-washings contribute to cumulative damage of even good quality clothes. Anyone with a shrunken cashmere sweater from machine-washing knows what I mean.

Your clothes suffer laundry-related damage from machine agitation (in the washer and dryer), over-washing, and heat (from hot water and hot dryers). When your clothes spin in a washer, they get some damage, and they get even more when they spin in your dryer. Don't believe me? Check your lint tray and you'll find all the proof you need. All that dust in the dryer lint tray is accumulated fibers from micro tears as clothes tumble dry. Hot water fades clothes, and the heat from the dryer shrinks clothes. Add to that a tendency to wash clothes more frequently than they need to be, and it becomes evident how laundering clothes can be a source of damage.

REMEMBER

The point is that laundry habits need to be designed to minimize damage to garments so that they can last longer.

In this section, I clue you in on how to do your laundry sustainably and in a way that minimizes laundry-related damage, keeping your clothes in good condition longer.

Making sense of labels

Before you wash your clothes, you need to check the label for instructions. Labels let you know whether the clothes are machine-washable or must be hand-washed or dry-cleaned and whether they can be tumble dried or must be line dried.

I get it — the symbols, the lack of words, and the random crosses on your clothing labels can be confusing. As dizzying as they are, you really need to try to understand them so that you can follow them. Otherwise, you'll end up shrinking or ruining the shape of your clothes. Sustainable brands tend to make deciphering labels much easier. They typically have care instructions clearly written in words as well as additional information on their website that's super helpful, but mass-produced clothes are likely to have only symbols and no clearly written instructions.

When buying clothes, make it a habit to look at the care instructions on the labels. These labels usually include symbols to illustrate how you should care for the item. Watch for words like "dry-clean only" and crossed-out symbols that mean things like "don't tumble dry," as these are the dos and don'ts. Otherwise, you could ruin your fab outfit in just one wash. By checking the care instructions before you buy clothes, you can decide at the time of purchase whether you can (or want to) handle the care. Figure 10-1 shows you what common laundry symbols look like and mean.

© Adobe Stock

FIGURE 10-1: A sample laundry chart to help demystify laundry symbols.

Some common laundry symbols include

>> **Washing symbols:** These describe whether you should hand-wash, dry-clean, or machine-wash the fabric. For machine-washing, you will see dots or actual temperature specifications; these are instructions on water temperature but just expressed differently. For the dots, one dot means cold wash, two dots mean warm wash, and three dots mean hot wash.

REMEMBER

Temperature specifications don't mean that you must wash at the specified temperature. It just means that the fabric can withstand the specified temperature.

Temperatures are usually written in Celsius, not Fahrenheit.

>> **Tumble drying symbols:** These provide instructions on how much heat the fabric can withstand.

>> **Drying symbols:** These explain how to line dry your clothes. Instructions on whether you should drip dry or dry flat, hang dry, and more. Wool sweaters, for example, should be dried flat.

>> **Ironing instructions:** These provide instructions on how much heat the fabric can handle or if you should avoid ironing the garment.

>> **Bleach symbols:** Should you bleach it? These symbols provide instructions on types of bleach you can use or whether you should avoid bleach. (For more eco-friendly ways to remove stains, read the "Removing Stains" section.)

>> **Crossed-out symbols:** These are instructions on what you definitely shouldn't do. For example, sweaters and silks shouldn't be put in the dryer.

TIP

Print a laundry label chart and keep it in your laundry room for easy reference.

Understanding washer settings

Sometimes, all those buttons and settings on the washing machine can seem unnecessarily confusing. Unfortunately, if you don't use the right settings, your indispensable laundry machine may ruin your clothes. If your clothes are spinning around in the machine longer than necessary, the chances of damage are much higher. Laundry machines generate very high temperatures, which damage clothes. On the flipside, hand-washing causes much less damage (see the section "Hand-washing delicates, sweaters, and more" for hand-washing tips and motivation).

Given how most of us live and how busy we are, it would be unrealistic to expect that more than a small number of us can make hand-washing a regular part of our routine, but this means that it's super important that you use the right settings on your machines for the fabric and design of the clothes you are laundering.

When setting up a laundry cycle, most people probably just fudge around and select the normal/cotton setting, play around with the temperature or timer, and let the machine do its thing. But that's not a good idea. I think the normal setting (regular or cotton on some machines) is quite misleading because it's just not appropriate for all clothes; use of the word "normal" may make you assume that it's appropriate for all your fabrics, but it's certainly not a good setting for clothes you consider delicate. The normal cycle generates very high heat and has a fast spin setting. The normal setting is good for some garments, such as heavy-duty cotton pants, soiled clothes, but may not be appropriate for a finer cotton T-shirt.

Washer settings are labeled differently by brand of machine but are essentially the same. They are just about water temperature, speed of spin, and length of washing cycle.

REMEMBER

Keep the water cold and the cycle as short as possible when it comes to using washers.

Following is a handy list of ways to use your washer to minimize damage to your clothes:

» **Choose the shortest possible cycle.** If the clothes are not heavily soiled, there's no need for them to be spinning around for longer than necessary.

» **Use cold water.** Cold water slows fading and shrinking and is better for the environment. Some labels on your clothes may say wash in warm water, but that doesn't mean you have to; it just means the clothes can withstand high heat. Unless you must sanitize, cold water is fine. Also, most modern laundry detergents have been formulated to work with cold water, so the hot water recommendation is old news.

>> **Be wise about how you choose settings.** The normal setting is a high heat and fast spin setting and isn't always necessary. I prefer permanent press for my non-delicates; it uses less heat and produces less wrinkling. Don't forget to use cold water; most new machines allow you to adjust water temperature settings.

>> **Wash colored fabrics inside out.** This way the non-colored part takes the beating, preserving the color on the outside from fading.

>> **Sort by fabric.** People typically sort by color, but sorting by fabric is important too. A white delicate blouse should not be washed with white towels. Clothes made of heavy material may tear or rip clothes that are thin and lightweight if they're washed together.

>> **Wash delicates in a mesh bag.** They'll take less of a beating as the washer spins.

>> **Use only gentle settings for sweaters.** It's better to hand-wash sweaters and avoid the washer, as machine agitation and heat shrinks sweaters. But if you use the washer, use the hand-wash setting, cold water, and a mesh bag for more protection from friction. Don't wash sweaters with heavy fabrics. Even though a sweater may be labeled machine-washable, you still have to take extra care when washing it in a machine. And make sure to air-dry sweaters flat after a machine-wash.

Hand-washing delicates, sweaters, and more

Hand-washing is much gentler on clothes than machine-washing and helps clothes last longer, but for most people it may not be practical. I take myself as an example: I have hand-washed pretty much everything, from sheets to underwear, but it's not something I can realistically do for all my clothes or all the time. But I recommend hand-washing your delicates, wools, swimwear, activewear, and bras.

REMEMBER

Yes, there are hand-wash settings on washing machines, but even those cycles can damage clothes. They use energy, which may conflict with your efforts to conserve and live an environmentally friendly lifestyle. If you're looking for the safest option for your clothes and to conserve energy, real hand-washing is the way to go.

OUTSMARTING THE SOCK-EATING MONSTER

Many of us have determined that our laundry machines are a necessary evil. We know they use a lot of water and energy, but did you know that they lead to laundry pileups in landfills? Fortunately, you can minimize both of these effects.

So how do washers create landfill waste? Somehow washers and dryers seem to eat up socks, forcing us to buy more. It's not your imagination; your socks indeed disappear, and there are plausible explanations — either the socks get lost in transit to the laundry or get stuck in the machines. But regardless of the reason, we end up sending lots of partnerless socks to landfills as a result. You can avoid this by rolling the socks together, or by using binder clips or safety pins. Machines are already doing a lot of damage to your garments; don't let them eat your socks too!

Activewear and swimsuits pick up a lot of odors from sweat and chlorine. Washing them immediately keeps these odors at bay. So just hand-wash them immediately. Hand-washing also helps them retain shape longer.

REMEMBER

You can hand-wash almost everything — not only those items I am recommending you hand-wash. There are some obvious exceptions like leather, suede, and velvet that you can't hand-wash or throw into a washing machine. But it's important to know that just because an item has a machine-washable label doesn't mean you have to go that route; it just means you can.

Drying clothes differently

A lot of people use machine dryers to dry their laundry, and although dryers may seem to make the laundry process simpler, they aren't great for clothing longevity. Dryers cause shrinkage and small micro-tears in your clothes. Dryers shrink clothes twice as much as washers. It's not the temperature of a tumble dryer that causes shrinkage — it's the agitation and forced air that affects the fabric's size. As your clothes tumble, this same agitation of tumble drying produces microscopic wear, which is the lint you see at the end of a drying cycle! But there are ways to minimize or prevent this damage, which means your clothes will be in circulation longer — a sustainability dream come true.

Using the good old air-dry method

Air-drying is an easy and effective way to get your clothes dry. It's very common in many parts of the world; just check dreamy photos from European vacations and you will see clothes hanging on balconies. I probably air-dry 60 percent of my clothes and love how air-drying keeps my clothes in great shape.

REMEMBER

Air-drying is far less damaging to your clothes. There is none of that fabric loss that you see in lint trays. It's even better for white clothes as the UV rays from the sun brighten your whites. Air-drying is not only friendlier to your clothes but is also eco-friendly because it doesn't require any electricity. Now that's sustainable!

I live in a city in the United States and don't have a backyard, so I use a drying rack in my bathroom. It isn't a cultural norm to use terraces or balconies to air-dry clothes (like in many cities around the world), ergo, my bathroom. Air-drying can seem impractical, but it is doable. All you need is a collapsible rack and pegs. Here are some tips to make air-drying work for you.

>> Improve air circulation so clothes dry faster by using a fan or dehumidifier if humidity is preventing your clothes from drying.

>> To help your clothes dry faster, don't air-dry clothes that are soaking wet. Instead, roll them up in a towel first, to help remove some of the water. This helps with drying clothes indoors faster, since you don't have the sun or wind to speed things up.

>> Space clothes out and don't lay them on top of each other. They dry faster that way.

>> Put less laundry in each load. This helps with space issues. If you don't have a lot of room, you won't be able to hang all the clothes in your load.

>> Reshape the garment while it's damp so it dries that way.

Using a dryer

If you prefer to use a dryer machine instead of air-drying your clothes, then you'll want to know how to minimize the damage.

I admit that I still use a dryer for certain items, like socks, pajamas, older clothes I wear at home, and sheets and towels (because I have limited line drying space for the bigger items).

Over-drying your clothes leads to shrinkage and weakening of the fabric. Always choose a lower heat setting even if it takes a little longer to dry your clothes. Your machine's standard setting is probably too hot.

If your clothes are not dry enough when you get them out of the dryer, air-dry them to achieve desired dryness outside the dryer (call this a hybrid method if you like). Alternatively, if those items will need to be ironed, iron them while they are still damp. The moisture provides a natural steam effect, and the wrinkles disappear faster.

TIP

I have always ironed my clothes inside out, as an additional step to keep them in good shape. I'm always nervous about marks and burns. These things happen, but it's better if they occur on the inside of your clothes. You can also use a press cloth!

Another thing you can do is use wool dryer balls to help clothes dry faster in the dryer (I prefer them to dryer sheets that have chemicals in them). They speed up drying by preventing clothes from clumping together and allowing air to circulate better. Don't have dryer balls? Give your clothes a good shake when you take them out of the washer so they're not clumped together, and they will dry faster.

REMEMBER

Sweaters should not go into the dryer, even machine-washable ones. If this is all you take away from this section, you will save yourself from the annoyance of shrunken sweaters.

Keeping clothes fresh without over-washing

Do you wash your clothes after wearing them once? Many people do, but that's not always necessary. Some clothes don't require frequent washing. Your jeans don't have to be washed after every use; you can go up to ten wears before a wash. Obviously, you need to wash your clothes, but washing clothes too frequently can mean premature wear and tear. In addition to jeans, trousers and skirts don't need to be washed after one wear. Generally, with clothes that don't cling tight to your body — the more loose-fitting ones — you can skip a wash. And who doesn't want to spend less time doing laundry? Your linen dresses don't need washing often because linen is breathable and doesn't get as sweaty as activewear or a polyester blouse that traps oil and sweat.

So if you aren't washing your jeans or loose-fitting dresses after every wash, you may be concerned about odors or small dirty spots. Worry not. There are ways to keep your clothes fresh between washes:

>> **Spot-clean your clothes.** You don't have to wash a dress just because of a small spill; get into the habit of spot-cleaning.

>> **Air out your clothes after wearing them.** Don't put clothes away immediately even if they aren't sweaty. Let them air out in your bathroom or bedroom. If you have space outside, let them hang in the sun for a little while; the UV rays will sanitize the clothes for you.

>> **Freshen them up with a steamer.** You know steamers get rid of wrinkles, but they can also freshen up your clothes. The heat from the steamed water kills odor-causing bacteria.

>> **Spray 'em clean.** There are freshening sprays on the market, but most have toxic ingredients, so use vodka instead. Put some cheap vodka in a spray bottle and spray a small amount on your clothes to remove odors. Don't worry, vodka is odorless, so you won't smell like a bar (but don't try this with gin). This is a trick used by stage performers as they can't always wash or dry-clean costumes between performances.

>> **Brush your fabrics.** Throwing clothes with lint, fuzz, and hair into the wash isn't necessary; you just need to give them a good brushing. Gently brush the clothes with a clothes brush to gently freshen and neaten them.

Deciding on dry-cleaning

Yet another way to clean clothes is to send them to the dry cleaner. Some people rarely go to the dry cleaner, and others send their clothes there a few times a month. But for most people, the dry cleaner can seem like a magical place shrouded in mystery. You give the dry-cleaning employee your clothes, and poof! In a few days they're like new.

Dry-cleaning has its positives when it comes to garment care, but unfortunately, it is also associated with some environmental concerns and, of course, additional costs. A toxic chemical, perchloroethylene (PERC), is used in dry-cleaning and is a known health and environmental hazard. Its use is generally regulated, although enforcement is quite a different matter in many places.

I have met some dry cleaners who are voluntarily working on moving away from it, but it's still widely used. There are also dry cleaners that offer green cleaning, which is essentially professional wet-cleaning without the use of PERC. It works by washing clothes at varying degrees of mechanical agitation based on fabric, so they don't shrink. Many of your clothes, such as dress shirts, can be green cleaned. For items that can't be wet-cleaned, ask your dry cleaner if they use alternatives to PERC.

Until the industry evolves to a point where all the environmental concerns associated with dry-cleaning can be addressed, my recommendation is that you dry-clean clothes only when the fabric label indicates that dry-cleaning is necessary. (Read the earlier section "Making sense of labels" for more on laundry labels.)

REMEMBER

Many pieces that you may think are dry clean only, like silks and linens, can also be hand-washed. If a garment has the dry-clean only symbol, you might be able to get away with washing it yourself; you'll will need to wash these items very carefully and gently. Otherwise, you may ruin your garments. Some fabrics may be prone to color bleeding, shrinking, or texture changes.

I avoid dry-cleaning only clothes that need to be washed often, but I do dry-clean my really special clothes occasionally. For example, I have a beautiful linen dress, handmade and with beautiful embroidery — not an everyday dress, but one which I wear occasionally. When it needs washing, I send it to the dry cleaners because I really love it, I spent a pretty penny on it, and I don't wear it enough that it becomes expensive to dry-clean.

TIP

If you really want to avoid the dry cleaners, don't purchase "dry-clean only" clothes! Check the care instructions on clothes before you buy them. If the item is labeled "dry-clean only," put it back on the shelf.

Caring for Different Fabrics

Fabrics not only look different, but they also react differently to heat and water. Some fabrics are more sensitive, and others can pack a punch with limited damage. In this section, I share what to do with clothes of all different fabrics so that everything in your closet lasts for years.

Cleaning your cotton clothes

Cotton is a natural, versatile, soft fabric that's easy to take care of. It is generally machine-washable but it's prone to shrinkage and wrinkling.

TECHNICAL
STUFF

Why does cotton shrink? Cotton is made from plant fibers that are stretched (tension is applied) into yarn and then woven into cotton fabric. The heat from the washer — and even more so the dryer — relaxes that tension, causing the fabric to shrink.

You can prevent your cotton clothes from shrinking by avoiding excessive heat. Wash cotton clothes in cold water and air-dry them when possible. If you must use the dryer, use low heat and take clothes out when they're still damp, which will prevent over-drying and wrinkling. Most detergents work well for cotton, but mild eco-friendly detergents are gentler. Cotton is safe to iron; consider using a low- to medium-heat setting and a pressing cloth, or iron inside out.

Avoiding shrinking your wools

Wools can shrink down three sizes when put in the dryer. This shrinkage is caused by the heat and agitation in the washer and dryer, so hand-washing is an easy way to prevent your wools from shrinking.

TECHNICAL
STUFF

Wool fibers are made from protein scales, so a combination of heat and agitation makes the scales expand and catch on each other, which binds the fibers closer together. As the fibers get closer, they shrink.

Hand-wash wool in cool water using a mild, wool-appropriate detergent. Should you put them in the washer, select a delicate setting with cold water and put them in a mesh bag or pillowcase for extra protection. Wool should be air-dried flat, because line-drying or drying on hangers will stretch out the wool. You can iron wool on very low heat if you need to.

HOW TO UNSHRINK WOOL

If you've ever washed your wool improperly, you're familiar with the consequences: a shrunken garment that makes you wonder if you packed on some pounds overnight. Fortunately, you don't need to donate or trash that wool garment just yet. You can unshrink wool! Save your sweater by following these steps:

1. Fill a bathroom sink with lukewarm water and ½ cup of hair conditioner.

2. Let your sweater soak in the solution for 10–15 minutes to unlock the wool fibers.

3. Let the water out, but don't wring or rinse the sweater. Just press it against the sides of the sink to remove excess water.

4. Lay the sweater flat between two towels and press gently to remove more water.

5. Stretch the sweater to its original size. It's easier if you have some help. Just place the sweater against your chest and have someone stretch it until it's your size.

6. Air-dry the sweater flat.

This method works only if the wool is not *felted* (fibers have become matted). The agitation and heat of the machine that shrink wool can cause felting. Felting changes both the size and texture, creating a dense fuzzy fabric, and this can't be reversed. But you can still give that wool a purpose (and make a sustainable choice), because felted wool can be used for crafting. Reuse that wool to create something new.

Removing and preventing pilling

Although mostly seen in wool, all fabric pills. The small balls of fuzz you see on clothes are from pilling. Wool has the most pilling because it has looser fibers. Thankfully, a lot of the washing methods discussed in this section can help reduce the amount of pilling, but you probably can't completely prevent it. Pilling is a natural process that occurs from wear as fibers brush against each other when you're moving, so it's helpful if you know what to do when it happens. Don't give up on your clothes — you can remove the fuzz easily with the proper tools and methods. The most efficient way to remove pilling is to use a fabric shaver or lint remover.

REMEMBER

A better-quality wool sweater will pill less than a poorer quality one, because a better-quality sweater will be made from longer fibers that are woven tight. Nevertheless, *all* sweaters will pill to some extent because it's just the nature of wool. If you want to keep your sweaters for a long time, as you should, you have to do a little fuzz removal. I find it to be oddly satisfying.

Saving your silks

Silk is delicate and prone to color loss and water staining. Dry-cleaning silk is probably the best way to extend its life, but it can totally be hand-washed with *care* in cool water with mild detergent, preferably those made for silks and delicates. Heritage Park and Ethique Laundry Bar are examples of clean detergents you can use for washing silk. Hand-washing silk should be done quickly (but gently) as you don't want to expose the silk to water for an extended period. Silk items should be drip-dried.

TIP

Since silk is delicate and expensive, a low-stress way to get that luxury feel is to buy silks secondhand. Secondhand items are more affordable and better for the environment, so you can feel good (instead of guilty) about buying yourself pre-owned silks.

Chasing the moths away

When it comes to things that ruin your clothes, moths eating them is a super upsetting one. It's actually not the moths that eat your clothes but rather their larvae, which are hard to see. Before you go panicking at the sight of any moths, there are only two types of moths whose larvae will eat your clothes: the case-making clothes moth (*Tinea pellionella*) and the webbing clothes moth (*Tineola bisselliella*).

TECHNICAL STUFF

If you have been buying clothes made from cotton or synthetics, you probably haven't had to worry about moths before. Not all fabrics are the favorite cuisine of these hungry larvae. They mostly feed on keratin found in animal fibers, including knitwear, such as wool and cashmere, as well as fur, leather, and feathers. They rarely feed on cotton and synthetics unless they are soiled with food, body oils, or blended with animal fibers.

Preventing moths

Moths like dark places with little movement or few disturbances, so they're likely to be found around clothes that are stored away. Their larvae thrive in humid, dirty conditions, so think of sweaty, unlaundered clothes in dark places and humid spots like your basements.

Now that you know where they're likely to be and what they eat, here are some tips on keeping moths away:

>> Wash clothes before you store them.

>> Store clothes you are not wearing in airtight containers or freezer bags.

>> Use cedar (blocks, chests, drawers) or lavender oils or pouches as these repel moths.

REMEMBER

These methods can prevent a moth infestation, but they can't fix an existing one.

Mothballs are effective in preventing moth infestations, but they contain pesticides and can be toxic to children and pets.

WARNING

Dealing with an infestation

If you spot moths, inspect your clothes for infestation and look for holes in them. Get rid of all the infested clothes and then wash clothes that are not infested. Dry-cleaning is considered very effective at killing any larvae. This may sound expensive, but it's better than have a full-scale moth invasion on your hands. If the problem is really bad, bring in pest control.

Making synthetics last

Synthetics like polyester are unsustainable fabrics (see Chapter 3 for the lowdown on commonly used synthetics). Sadly, a lot of synthetics are out there in retail and thrift stores, and given that synthetics take up to 1,000 years to decompose, taking care of them is important to keep them out of landfills. Synthetic fabrics also shed *microplastics*, which are tiny plastic pollution, specifically small plastic pieces that less than 5 millimeters long. (For more on reducing microplastic pollution, see the nearby sidebar.) If you own clothing made from synthetic materials (and you probably do), it's important to make those clothes last!

REDUCING MICROPLASTICS

Microplastics enter our environment, water, food supplies, and (eventually) our bodies in many ways. One of those ways is through laundering synthetic garments. Studies have shown that a single load of laundry releases roughly 700,000 microplastics, roughly about the size of a pack of gum. (For more on the fashion industry and microplastics, check out Chapter 3.)

Fortunately, you can reduce the microplastics shed by your clothes.

- Wash your synthetic clothes in a Guppyfriend laundry bag. Put your synthetic garments in this bag before you toss them into the washing machine. While these bags don't trap all microplastics, they help reduce the amount shed into the water supply.

- Use a Cora ball. This is a laundry ball that you toss into the laundry with your synthetics. The Cora ball helps prevent microplastics from shedding from your clothes.

- Attach microfiber filters to your washing machine. Filters like Planet Care help prevent microplastics from your laundry from getting into our rivers.

- Use cold water and faster cycles.

These methods aren't foolproof, but they do help to limit microplastic shedding. Perhaps if more of us use them, we can make a positive impact.

Polyester is relatively easy to maintain, so no excuses! It's machine-washable and won't shrink in the dryer, but it's prone to pilling, so wash your polyester clothes inside out. Nylon can be washed in the washing machine, but it's prone to static so skip the dryer and air-dry it instead. Workout clothes are made from spandex, which holds onto odors, so hand-wash them immediately after a wear. (New to hand-washing? Check out "Hand-washing delicates, sweaters, and more.")

Loving your linens

Linen is my favorite fabric; it's durable, and because it's breathable, it's lovely for summer wear. Contrary to popular belief, linen can be washed at home and does not need to be dry-cleaned.

I looked at the labels on my linen clothes and all of them indicate that the item can be hand-washed or machine-washed. I suggest hand-washing linen because it can shrink from the heat and agitation of the washer and dryer, similar to other fabrics. Souse a delicate cycle with cold water and then air-dry. Also, remember that anything that can be machine-washed can be hand-washed, so you should hand-wash your linen. Linen can withstand heat from an iron, and you'll need an iron because linen does wrinkle easily.

REMEMBER

It seems like a lot to do — read labels, understand fabrics, understand your machine settings, and so on — but I can assure you that it becomes second nature. One of the most sustainable things you can do is take care of items you already own so you don't have to buy new ones.

Removing Stains

No matter how careful you are, your clothes are likely to get a stain, and for young kids, it's a daily struggle. Stains are a nuisance, but help is on the way. Here's what you can do to get those pesky stains out of your beloved garments:

>> **Keep stain-removing products in your home at all times.** Stains are bound to happen, so have some stain-fighting supplies at home. If you have to run to the store the next day to buy supplies for stains, it will be harder to remove them, which can be frustrating if a favorite garment gets ruined.

>> **Work on removing stains immediately.** Fresh stains are much easier to remove than old ones.

>> **Air-dry stained clothing.** Don't put stained clothes in the dryer — this will make stains permanent.

>> **Be persistent and don't give up.** You may have to spend several minutes or even try several methods to remove a stain.

I struggle using most of what is usually recommended to fight stains because a lot of these products have a lot of chemicals, but thankfully, there are some natural nontoxic options that you may already have in your home. If you don't, get some and keep them handy. I recommend these:

- **Lemon juice/lime juice:** Fresh or bottled 100 percent lemon or lime juice has natural bleaching properties. It's great for yellow armpit sweat stains.

- **Distilled white vinegar:** This is another nontoxic natural bleach that works for yellowing, and it removes odors.

- **Corn starch:** You can use corn starch for oily/greasy stains.

- **Dish detergent:** Dishwashing liquid not only removes grease and oil on dishes but can also work for grease stains on clothes.

- **Hydrogen peroxide:** This works for a variety of stains, including red wine, veggies, juice stains, grass stains, dye transfer stains, blood, sweat, and odors.

Some eco-friendly commercial stain fighters are available if you are more comfortable with manufactured formulations.

REMEMBER

Deciding How to Store Your Clothes

To hang or to fold? That is the question. How you store your clothes really matters. Clothes need to be stored in the way that's best for the garment. Some clothes need to hang, and others need to be folded so they don't get too wrinkled, get stretched out, or lose their structure.

For example, the best way to maintain the shape of a collar is to hang your shirts buttoned up. It not only looks neater, but it's also better to keep them looking good and in shape. Heavy fabrics like your sweaters should be folded because on hangers they will get stretched out. By folding them, you're not only helping your clothes last longer but also making it easier for yourself with fewer wrinkles and lines that you must iron out.

The following sections guide you through what you should fold and what you should hang up in your closet.

Clothes you should hang

Some clothes are best put on hangers to help them maintain their shape and structure. These include the following:

>> **Collared blouses/shirts and jackets:** Hang them on a hanger that has a shape similar to that of the shoulders. Generally avoid metal hangers; they can cause pokes on the shoulders. Button up the shirts to maintain the shape of the collar.

>> **Dresses, jumpsuits, or anything flowy:** Flowy garments should be stored the way the fabric flows. Folding can remove pleats and create excessive wrinkling.

However, jumpsuits and dresses made from jersey fabric should be folded to avoid stretching.

>> **Pants and skirts:** Hang your skirts on hangers with clips. Dress pants should be folded along the crotch. This helps reduce creasing.

>> **Blazers and coats:** Choose hangers that are similar in shape to the shoulders to maintain their structure.

Clothes you should fold

Some clothes will stretch and lose shape if you place them on hangers. Fold them instead.

>> **Activewear:** Activewear will get stretched out on hangers.

>> **Sweaters:** Folding sweaters helps them maintain structure and not stretch out. It also saves you some closet space!

>> **T-shirts:** T-shirts will stretch on hangers, so fold them. You should stack them neatly as they can help you see what you have and avoid buying extra tees you don't need.

IN THIS CHAPTER

» **Playing your part in circular fashion**

» **Getting started on your first sewing project**

» **Repairing your own clothing**

» **Creating new clothes with upcycling**

» **Paying to have someone else fix it for you**

Chapter **11**

Repairing and Upcycling Your Clothes

Y ou don't have to buy your way into sustainable fashion because what you already own is the most sustainable fashion. As much as possible, avoid the continuous purchase of new garments or shoes and instead continue to find wears from the clothes and shoes you already own. Cherish the clothes you have and take care of them so they last longer in your closet and stay away from landfills.

A great way to make this happen is to mend them. Some minor repairs you can do yourself with just a few simple sewing techniques I show you in this chapter. I also introduce you to upcycling, which is a fun and creative way to give your old clothes a new life so they feel fresh and wearable again.

In this chapter, I guide you on how to show some love for your clothes that may not be in the best shape. I hope to inspire and guide you to get sewing and mending again if you have some prior experience, or get started if you're a first-timer. With some practice, you can do it!

Making Your Fashion Circular

You may have heard fashion brands use the term *circular fashion*. Circular fashion simply means circulating clothes responsibly and effectively in society for as long as possible and disposing of them only when they are no longer fit for use. Loads of wearable clothes are getting thrown away. Multiple sources have reported that in the United States, 85 percent of clothes end up in landfills. In that pile, there are probably clothes that may have just needed a little repair, such as fixing a ripped seam, replacing buttons, and so on. Therefore, circular fashion doesn't have to include a lofty or super complex plan. You can become an invaluable participant in the circularity movement from your own home by repairing and upcycling your own clothes.

You may be concerned by your lack of sewing skills, but thankfully, sewing is something most people can master. Sewing and mending went from something most people could do, being taught at home or at school, to something most people don't think of doing much anymore because of how easy it is to replace clothes. Fortunately, sewing is making a comeback, partly because of a shift toward eco-conscious consumption and the abundant inspiration seen on social media, where sewing bloggers and sewing enthusiasts showcase amazing sewing projects. Maybe you can jump on this wave too!

Challenge yourself to prioritize mending or investing in repairs that you can't do yourself. You may find it hard at the beginning, especially given that some fast fashion can be cheaper than the cost of professional tailoring services, and you may struggle to find the time to do it yourself. But as you practice, you'll get small repairs done quicker, and you may even find more challenging repairs like patching fulfilling and a new creative outlet.

REMEMBER

A stitch in time really saves nine and diminishes the chance that you will throw clothes away. Simple repairs are typically all you need to keep your clothes in circulation longer. Mending the clothes you already own is one of the most sustainable things you can do.

Getting Your Thread Wet

Eager as you may be, you shouldn't just grab a needle and stab your blazer. This section provides you with what you need to know, from moistening the thread tip to embarking on your first real repair. It includes a list of supplies you'll need (which does include a needle), and steps to take to get your supplies ready for action.

Prepping your sewing kit

For all your simple at-home mending, you'll be hand-sewing, so no need to worry about buying and storing the monstrous sewing machine your grandma brags about. You'll only need to do some basic mending yourself. The more complex repairs that require significant alterations can be taken to a tailor. So take a breath!

To get started, you need a few supplies. Thankfully, sewing supplies are widely available and inexpensive. You can buy sewing kits that have some basic supplies or put your own kit together.

TIP

Try to have your supplies with you ahead of time; you're more likely to mend if you have the tools you need at home. Otherwise, mending joins the pile of to-dos that you may never get around to, and then one fateful day, you may just throw them away, especially if you're in decluttering mode.

Your sewing kit should have the following:

>> **Thread in an assortment of colors:** Make sure you have white, black, navy, beige, and gray, as these will match most clothes you have.

>> **Needles:** You will use these to carry the thread through the fabric.

>> **Scissors:** Sharp scissors are all you need, but some sewing kits may come with mini scissors for cutting thread.

>> **Thimble (optional):** This handy device protects your fingers from getting poked by the needle.

>> **Pins:** You need these to help hold the fabric in place while you're sewing.

>> **Seam ripper:** Sometimes you may need to take some stitches out, and this tool makes it easier.

I got my first sewing kit at my local drugstore. I bought my first sewing kit when I urgently needed to sew a button back on my son's costume for a school performance. I rushed to the local drugstore and was pleasantly surprised to find out that it carried sewing kits. Actually, sewing kits are easy to find. I hadn't sewn a button in years, but there I was with my first sewing kit. I felt ready and able to take on the world — the world of sewing! It was a simple, portable, travel-size kit, but that's all you need for simple repairs. I try to have sewing supplies handy at all times.

Stitching up for sewing success

If you've never sewn before, the following tips will help get you started. All you need is your thread, needle, and scissors to cut the thread. These steps explain how to thread your needle and how to tie a starting knot and secure your stitches. They may sound simplistic, but you can't sew without knowing how to do them.

>> **Threading a needle:** You need to know how to thread a needle. If you're like me, this can take forever, especially if the needle eye is small. But the more you practice, the better you'll get at doing it. Just make sure you moisten the thread between your lips before you begin and cut the thread with sharp scissors so it has a blunt edge.

TIP

If you have poor eyesight or slippery fingers, you can use a needle threader. Most sewing kits have one. They look like metal coins. Be sure to handle them gently as they're usually a bit fragile.

>> **Making a starting knot:** You need to tie a simple knot at the end of your thread to secure the stitches. This is the *starting knot*. It catches the fabric so your stitches don't come undone as you sew.

Loop the short tail end of your thread over the longer side. Bring the short tail end through the loop and tighten the knot. One knot might not be big enough to catch the fabric, so you might have to do a couple of knots.

>> **Securing the stitching at the end:** You also need to secure your stitches once you are done sewing. You don't want all your hard work to unravel.

Place the needle under the last stitch but don't pull the thread out completely; instead, pull the thread till a loop forms. Pass the needle through the loop and pull the thread to tighten the knot. Repeat to create another knot. It may sound complex, but it's not. See Figure 11-1 to see how it is done. Cut the hanging threads neatly. Your stitches are secured!

FIGURE 11-1: Use this technique to secure your stitches.

Repairing Your Clothes with Basic Hand-Stitching

Now to the good part! There are lots of stitches, but I stick to the basics to get you started. You need to know the running stitch and the backstitch for the repairs discussed in this chapter. I guide you on how to sew a button, fix a ripped seam, patch a threadbare spot on your knits, and fix snagged clothes.

TIP

Sewing takes a little practice. YouTube has numerous tutorials that can help you get better at sewing and mending.

Using a running stitch

The running stitch is the easiest and probably the one that comes to mind when you think of sewing. You use this type of stitch to patch threadbare spots in your sweaters and socks. Threadbare spots occur when fabric gets weak and damaged from wear, resulting in some exposed threads or holes. You can also use the running stitch for quick temporary repairs, and you need to know how to do it before you move on to the backstitch, which is a much stronger stitch.

Thread your needle and make a knot (see the earlier section "Stitching up for sewing success"). Push the needle through the fabric from the back to the front and repeat this motion (back to front then front to back again) to create small, evenly spaced stitches as shown in Figure 11-2. The stitches will look like a dotted line when you are done.

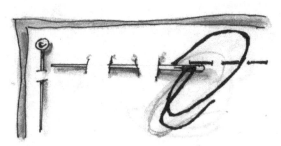

FIGURE 11-2: The running stitch is a foundational stitch. Use it for patching threadbare spots in your knits.

Doing the backstitch

The backstitch is similar to the running stitch except that there's less space between the stitches. The stitches look closer to a straight line, as shown in Figure 11-3, versus the dotted line of the running stitch. It's the strongest hand-stitch, so you use it for more durable repairs like fixing a ripped seam.

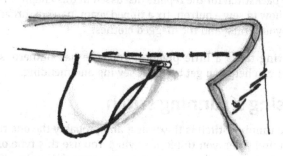

FIGURE 11-3: The backstitch is a sturdy hand-stitch. Use it for fixing seams.

REMEMBER

Most simple repairs can be done by hand; you don't have to get a sewing machine. The more complex repairs can be taken to tailors.

Follow these steps to do this stitch:

1. **Thread your needle and tie a knot.**

2. **Bring the needle up from the back of the fabric to the front of the fabric.**

3. **Re-insert the needle into the fabric from the front of the fabric to the back of the fabric about a quarter of an inch away.**

   This is your first stitch.

4. **Now bring your needle up from the back of the fabric to the front but move ahead a distance the same length as the first stitch.**

   (It's like you're skipping ahead, but you'll be sewing backward to fill this gap in the next step.)

5. **Re-insert the needle into the fabric from the front of the fabric to the back at the point where the first stitch ends.**

   This is the second stitch.

6. **Repeat what you did for the first stitch and then the second stitch until you finish the length of your seam.**

TIP

Practice these stitches on scrap fabric before you do a real repair. The first few times you practice, you may need to draw some straight lines in pencil on your scrap fabric to use as a guide on where to sew.

REMEMBER

Smaller and shorter stitches are stronger and tighter. Longer stitches are weaker and looser. When you are sewing, try to make stitches as close together as possible, so your repair work holds.

Sewing on a button

Losing a button or having a loose button is inevitable. Thankfully, it's one of the easiest repairs to make.

To sew a button, you need the following:

>> Two needles or one needle and a toothpick
>> Thread
>> A button

» Scissors

» A seam ripper (optional)

Here are the simple steps to sew a button:

1. **Remove the loose button.**

   You can use scissors but be careful not to cut your fabric. Alternatively, you can use a seam ripper, which won't damage the fabric.

2. **Thread your needle and make a knot.**

3. **Find the spot of the original button, and sew an X.**

   Start sewing from the back to the front and continue until you have sewn an X. (You will sew your button on this X. The X shows you where to place the button (see Figure 11-4a).

4. **Place the button on top of the X and place your second needle or toothpick on top of the button.**

   This may seem odd, but it helps create a shank to ensure that your button will get through the buttonhole without being sewed firmly to the fabric (see Figure 11-4b).

5. **Sew the button over the second needle or toothpick.**

   Sew an X, just as you did for the button placeholder. Continue making X's until the button is secure; typically, sewing about six times through each hole is good.

6. **Remove the second needle or toothpick.**

7. **Make the shank.**

   This creates space between the garment and the button so that the button is easier to fasten. To do it, push the needle up to the front and then take the thread and wrap it around the button about six times (see Figure 11-4c). Don't overdo it, or your shank will be too thick and visible.

8. **Make a knot to secure the button.**

   Pull the needle through the fabric to the back of the button (as close as possible to the stitches). Pull the needle through the thread at the back of the button and use the loop to create a knot. Do this a couple of times and your button should be firmly attached.

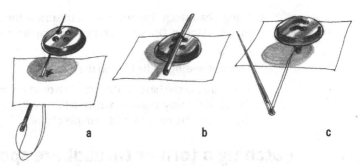

a   b   c

FIGURE 11-4: How to sew a button step by step: (a) Sew an X to help guide you where to place the button. (b) Use a spacer to help you make a thread shank in the next step. (c) Wrap the thread around the button six times to create the thread shank.

Repairing a seam

A seam is where two pieces of fabric are joined together; to fix a seam, sew the pieces back together. Not-so-funny story: Years ago, when I worked at a bank, I had the seam of my pants rip on me at work, and a customer noticed and let me know.

This is a repair you'll probably have to do at some point, either by yourself or by taking it to a tailor. To repair a seam, you need

>> Thread in the same color as the fabric

>> A needle

>> Sewing pins

Follow these simple steps to repair a ripped seam:

1. **Turn the garment inside out.**
   Sewing on the inside prevents the stitches from being visible.

2. **Pin the two pieces of fabric together at the rip to help guide your sewing.**

3. **Sew the seam using the backstitch method.**
   Refer to the earlier section "Doing the backstitch" and Figure 11-3. The backstitch is easy to do and strong enough to hold the seams together.

   • Start sewing a bit away from the rip. This helps you follow the line the rest of the seam helps secure your stitches.

- Using a backstitch, follow the line of the rest of the seam that is still intact. Use small stitches because they will be stronger.

- Continue sewing a little beyond the tear.

- To secure the stitching, on the last stitch don't pull the thread all the way. Leave a loop, take the needle through the loop, and tighten. Do this a couple of times.

Patching a torn or threadbare spot

You may be one of many who have a sweater or socks with holes in them. You can hold off throwing them away and patch these threadbare spots with a mending technique called darning. *Darning* is a sewing technique for repairing holes or worn areas in fabric or knitting using only a needle and thread.

Darning uses running stitches, so it's beginner friendly. You will make rows and columns of running stitches. I mention earlier that running stitches are not as strong as other stitches, but multiple rows are strong. Darning is visible mending; you won't be hiding the spots of repair. View it as a creative way to save your knits by adding some fun colors.

I was introduced to the world of darning recently, and I love watching videos of people fixing holes in sweaters and socks and adding fun colors for extra design. It feels so cozy, wholesome, and relaxing.

Darning requires different supplies from what you have in your sewing kit. Darning is mostly done on knits like socks and sweaters, so you need a different type of needle and thread.

>> **Darning yarn:** You need darning yarn instead of thread. Because darning is visible mending, you can use any color of your choice!

>> **Darning mushroom or darning egg:** A darning mushroom is a mushroom- or egg-shaped tool that is inserted into a knitted item to hold it in the proper shape and provide a stable surface for making repairs. You can also use a tennis ball!

>> **Darning needles:** These are different from regular needles. They are larger and have a dull, rounded tip.

>> **Pair of scissors:** You use scissors to cut the threads.

Follow these steps to repair the hole or threadbare patch:

1. **Place the darning mushroom under the hole for support.**

2. **Do vertical running stitches to cover the hole (see Figure 11-5a).**

   Space the stitches as close as possible. Stitches are stronger when they're closer together. Start sewing before the hole, sew until the hole is covered, and then extend past the hole.

3. **Repeat the Step 2 using horizontal running stitches.**

   See Figure 11-5b.

4. **To finish, pull the needle through the inside of the garment, stitch a few lines, and tie a knot.**

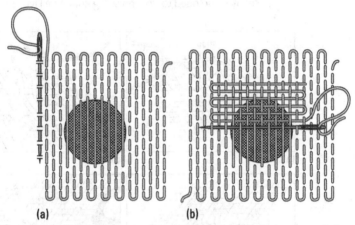

(a)   (b)

FIGURE 11-5: Darning to fix holes in your knits: (a) Sew vertical running stitches to cover the hole. (b) Sew horizontal vertical stitches to cover the hole.

Fixing snagged clothing

You've probably snagged your clothes by accidentally brushing against something sharp. Snags can ruin the appearance of your clothes, but fixing them is easy!

You need the following supplies:

>> **Thread:** Preferably the same color as the fabric.

>> **Needle:** Should be small or medium given that snags are small.

>> **Scissors:** Whatever kind you have handy will do.

Figure 11-6 shows you the steps. Here is what you need to do:

1. **Slip your needle and thread through the snag.**

   You don't need to knot the end of the thread when you thread the needle. See Figure 11-6a.

2. **Tie the thread to the snag and do a double knot.**

   See Figure 11-6b.

3. **Push the needle through the snag to the underside of the garment, pulling the snag through with it.**

   See Figure 11-6c.

4. **Turn the garment inside out and cut the excess thread.**

   And you are done! Remember you made the double knot already so no need to do a finishing knot. See Figure 11-6d.

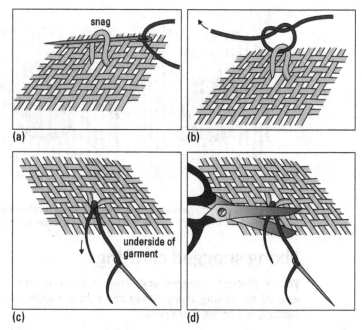

FIGURE 11-6: To fix snagged clothing, (a) slip the needle and thread through the snag, (b) do a double knot, (c) pull the snag through, and (d) cut excess thread.

REMEMBER

It's much easier to fix small tears before they become big ones, especially as a beginner. Check your clothes regularly for small rips, stains, or missing buttons. A good time to check is before you do laundry, or better still, as soon as you remove the clothes.

WARNING

Avoid washing clothes that have tears; instead, fix your torn clothes before you throw them into the washing machine. The agitation from the washer and dryer can make tears worse, making the item harder to repair.

Joining the Upcycling Movement

Upcycling is essentially turning worn-out pieces into fresh and wearable new pieces. It's a higher form of mending and keeping clothes alive longer. Stuff that would have been destined for landfills is made into something else that is valuable and desirable.

Upcycling always makes me think of the movie *The Sound of Music,* when Maria made outfits for the kids out of curtains. That was probably my first exposure to upcycling. I've seen people make dresses out of vintage sheets and old curtains. It's impressive. They turn fabric that otherwise would end up in landfills into something of higher value. It's a fun, creative way to reduce fashion waste.

There are a lot of upcycling projects you can do, and there are beginner-friendly ones that won't require sewing skills. If you can sew, the sky is the limit! You can make some great stuff out of old clothes and fabric.

Here are some ideas for simple upcycling projects that you can do by yourself!

Tie-dyeing your old shirts with avocado skins and pits

Tie-dyeing an old, stained white T-shirt can give it a new life! So don't throw it away; just give it a new color! And guess what? You can dye clothes with stuff you have at home like avocado skins and pits!

Tie-dyeing your old T-shirts with avocado skins and pits is an easy, inexpensive way to dye your T-shirts. It's also nontoxic!

You need the following:

>> A clean, old white T-shirt

>> Three to six avocado pits and skins (clean out all the green flesh)

>> A big pot

Proceed with these simple steps:

1. **Add avocado pits and skins to a pot of water and bring to a boil.**

2. **Simmer for about 30 to 60 minutes.**

3. **Wet your T-shirt, wring it dry, and then tie off sections with rubber bands.**

4. **Let the T-shirt sit in the dye bath overnight.**

5. **Remove the T-shirt from the dye bath, remove the rubber bands, and rinse it until the water runs clear.**

6. **Air-dry the T-shirt.**

The color will be pinkish. The intensity will vary based on how long you leave the T-shirt in the dye bath. If you want more color intensity, you can pretreat the T-shirt in a mordant like vinegar or soy milk.

If you want more color options, look for nontoxic dyes. Rit Dye has a great selection of nontoxic dyes for easy use at home.

Making old jeans new again

Cropping your old torn jeans or pants into shorts is a simple way to make something new and fresh out of something old.

Cropping and distressing your old jeans is a super easy DIY upcycle that doesn't require any sewing. All you need are

>> Scissors (fabric scissors if possible)

>> Old jeans

>> Tweezers

>> A razor

>> A measuring tape or another pair of shorts to use as a guide for the length you want

>> Tailor's chalk or white eyeliner to mark a line where you want to crop your jeans

The following sections walk you through how to crop and distress jeans.

Cropping the jeans

If your jeans have unwanted holes in the knees or are torn up at the bottom, cropping them is a great solution. Follow these steps to turn your old jeans into a new pair of shorts or cropped jeans:

1. **Lay the jeans on a flat surface.**

2. **Using either the tape measure or another pair of shorts, mark out your desired length with chalk or white eyeliner.**

3. **Cut on the line you drew in Step 2 with your fabric scissors.**

    Fold the jeans in half and cut both legs at once so you're sure that both sides are the same length.

TIP

4. **Get your razor and rub it along the cropped edges until they fray.**

    Fraying the edges creates a more finished look.

Distressing the jeans

Distressed, ripped-up denim has been in and out of style for decades. If your once-pristine jeans now sport a few holes, you can lean into the rough and edgy style by distressing them. You can do it in two simple steps:

1. **Decide where you want to have your distressing and cut a pair of small slits (parallel to each other).**

    Cut more slits if you want more distressing.

2. **Get your tweezers and pull out the blue threads that you see but leave the white threads.**

    Denim is made from weaving blue and white yarn. You create the distressing by pulling out the blue yarn and the white yarn left gives the distressed effect.

TIP

To make your distressed jeans look more authentic, you can fray the pockets. Get your scissors and cut very little fabric from the top of the pocket; then get your razor and fray the ends.

Investing in Alterations or Other Significant Repairs

Most of the clothes sold in stores are ready-to-wear and built to fit an average body type. This also means that many store-bought clothes won't fit you quite right because an "average" standard isn't representative of everyone. You've likely considered or done alterations. Wedding gowns are a good example of clothing that typically needs to be altered. The case of adjusting clothes for special occasions is clear, but it gets tricky for everyday clothes.

I get it — it's an additional cost, and you may feel like you can just get rid of it and get something that fits you better right off the rack. The decision to invest in alterations really depends on your personal equations. From a sustainability perspective, I would say yes to investing in fixing or adjusting your clothes. If something fits you well and flatters you, you'll probably be motivated to keep it longer. But alterations can range from affordable, such as adjusting the hem or replacing elastic, to hundreds of dollars for some bigger repairs or adjustments.

I think it boils down to what you are comfortable paying and how much you value the piece. Here are some things to consider to help guide your decision:

>> **The quality of the piece:** Quality pieces last a long time, so alterations may be worthwhile.

>> **How much you treasure the piece:** Your weight may have fluctuated, but if you still love the piece, you may be willing to pay to have it taken in or let out. Or maybe you have a vintage piece, handed down from family members.

>> **What purpose the garment serves:** Special occasion garments usually need to be altered. For example, most people are comfortable paying to alter a wedding dress; in fact, it should probably be part of the budget planning.

If you're up for getting your garment altered or repaired, you need to know who can help you get it done and where to find these talented people. The following sections give you the scoop on the world of tailoring and alterations.

Knowing what alterations specialists can help you with

A good professional tailor can fix almost everything that you can't repair yourself.

The following list points out some of the amazing things these talented people can do:

>> **Transform your clothes into a new style:** If you have a vintage piece that you want to bring into the current century, a good tailor can help you with that.

>> **Adjust the fit of your clothes:** They can make clothes smaller, let out clothes if they have big enough seam allowances, narrow shoulders, resize arm holes, shorten sleeves, and lots more.

>> **Replace zippers or loosen or tighten elastic:** You can have the elastic of your pants or skirts replaced by a professional. They can also replace old zippers for you.

>> **Fix flaws:** Mend a gaping blouse by adding a hidden snap.

Finding someone who does quality work

Because people are not repairing clothes as much as they used to, there may not be as many tailors as there were in the past, but you should be able to find one near you.

Here are a few strategies for finding a great tailor:

>> **Ask at the dry-cleaners:** Dry-cleaners are probably the easiest places to find tailors. Most have tailors who come in a couple of times a week. Start by giving them simple repairs and if you like their work, you can give them more complex jobs. Some of the tailors can be very good. I know of one who was poached by a top designer from a dry-cleaner.

>> **Word of mouth:** Asking people in your community or friends and family is a good way to find someone who does great work. If you're on a local community Facebook group, ask there. People will likely only recommend tailors who have done good work for them, so ask around.

>> **Google and Yelp:** Google "[tailor, or tailoring services] near me." The good thing about Yelp and Google is there may be reviews. People only give reviews if things are very good or very bad.

IN THIS CHAPTER

» **Maintaining and your leather shoes**

» **Taking care of your sneakers**

» **Protecting your shoes from water and stains**

» **Storing your shoes the right way**

Chapter **12**

Walking Miles in Your Favorite Shoes

My favorite pair of shoes — or perhaps I should call them the MVPs (most valuable players) of my shoe closet — are leather boots I bought about five years ago. The sales pitch to me had been that they were the sturdiest boots I was going to find at a relatively friendly price. I took that sales pitch literally, and for three years I wore them regularly with little care, telling myself they could take it, being the sturdiest boots; but they started to look dull, and some scuff marks started to build up.

At a point, I decided that I was not going to be able to wear them any longer without some restorative care. So I took them to a shoe shiner for a cleaning. I stayed and watched the shoe shiner take my shoes from dull to shiny cover up the scuff marks and return the shoes to their original beauty. I thanked the shoe shiner profusely. I also bought some shoe polish and a shoe brush, and five years later, I still have those boots. Not only was I able to keep on wearing my killer kicks for years to come, but I was living sustainably.

While I wouldn't say that shoe care at home is a dying practice, I believe that disposable fashion culture has caused people to be less likely to take the time to care for their shoes. People are repairing less, choosing instead to move on to the next pair and the pair after that, either because so many items are available or because they don't know how to properly care for their shoes.

This chapter aims to solve that problem. It tells you what you can do at home to prolong the life of the shoes you already own and why doing so is a big step toward a more sustainable lifestyle.

Considering Why Caring for Your Shoes Is a Shoo-In

You may be wondering what shoes have to do with your sustainable fashion journey. The truth is that footwear fashion has a big impact on the environment and garment workers around the world — which are key components of sustainability.

Americans throw away an estimated 300 million pairs of shoes annually, 95 percent of which end up in landfills where they take several decades to decompose. Leather shoes take 25–40 years, rubber takes 50–80 years, and shoes made from plastics take over 1,000 years to decompose. Conversations around sustainable fashion may seem to focus on clothes, but shoes are piling up in landfills too. So, taking care of your shoes is a great sustainable habit.

Shoes can be recycled, but this is most commonly done by down-cycling them into playground surfacing or carpet padding rather than by making them into new shoes. So even though recycling your shoes is better than dropping them in the trash, it's still not the best option.

So what is the best option? Keeping those shoes in tip-top condition so they can be used and reused for as long as possible. You have the power to make big changes to your waste footprint (pun intended) by taking small, easy steps. You can throw away fewer shoes if you take better care of the ones you already own.

Prolonging the Life of Your Leather Shoes

People have been wearing leather shoes for thousands of years. The oldest known shoe found in Armenia is estimated to be 5,000 years old, and it was still in great shape when it was found in 2008! Makes me hopeful that my leather shoes have a good chance of lasting me a long time — with the proper care, of course!

TIP

When you get a new pair of shoes, familiarize yourself with how to appropriately care for them. In general, caring for your leather requires minimal daily maintenance and occasional treatments and polishing.

Leather is a durable, sturdy fabric but is also quite sensitive; it's sensitive to the sun, harsh chemicals, and water. Excessive sun dries leather and makes it lose its natural oils, making it susceptible to cracking. Water dries out leather! Being a natural fabric, it's also sensitive to harsh chemicals. Once you know how to take care of your leather, you won't have to replace your shoes as often.

TECHNICAL
STUFF

Although leather is a natural fabric, it's not without environmental consequences. For more on the environmental impact of different fabrics, check out Chapter 5.

Everyday maintenance of leather shoes

You've probably owned a pair of leather shoes at some point, but do you keep leather-care products at home? Do you wipe them down before you put them away at the end of the day? Do you store them properly? If you don't do any of these things, you are certainly not alone. But simple shoe care can prolong the life of your shoes.

You may think leather shoes are supposed to be low maintenance, but they still require a little TLC every day. The following sections provide you with easy-peasy tips and tricks to better protect and care for your leather shoes.

Wipe down shoes after each use

This is probably the last thing on your mind at the end of a long day! Your shoes are probably cast aside as you get through the door. But try and remember to wipe down your shoes after each use with a soft cloth or shoe brush. This will keep them free from dust, as it spoils the leather over time, and it will also keep minor stains and scuffs at bay. Keep your brush and/or cloth close to your entrance so you can wipe your shoes immediately after you get home.

Treat all your leather shoes as you would treat your special shoes — they serve you every day, so they're clearly just as important as any special shoes you may have. Plus, it barely takes any time at all!

Avoid wearing leather in wet weather

Avoid wearing leather during a rain downpour or on snowy days, as both water and salt on sidewalks will damage your shoes. Water dries leather out. The natural oils in leather bind to water molecules, and when the water evaporates, it draws out the oil. This makes the shoes become stiff, brittle, and prone to cracking. Water also can stain leather or cause streaking. In winter months I used to leave my dress shoes at the office and wear a pair of weather-appropriate shoes to deal with the elements during my commute (using public transportation in New York City). Doing this helped me prolong the life of my leather shoes.

If you live in a place with unpredictable weather or where it rains on and off all the time, you may want to consider waterproofing your leather shoes (see "Using Shoe Protectants").

WARNING

If you use a waterproofing spray, choose an eco-friendly one, so that you are not solving one problem but exacerbating another, that of chemical pollution.

TIP

There is always a chance that your shoes will get wet while you're out and about, especially given that weather forecasts are never perfect. But there are steps you can take to prevent your shoes from getting completely ruined, including the following:

>> Towel dry your shoes to remove any water.

>> Remove the insoles if possible and stuff the shoes with a newspaper or any other used paper, as this can help dry the inside of the shoes.

   Leather shoes are sensitive to the sun and heat in general, so don't put them out in the sun or near a heater to dry. Let the shoes dry slowly in a room-temperature space.

>> Once dry, apply a leather conditioner finish. (For more on polishing and conditioning, see the section "Occasional maintenance of your leather shoes.")

>> Lastly, use a waterproofing spray or lotion to protect your shoes for next time.

Rotate your shoes daily

You may love your mid-calf leather combat boots, but don't love them to death by wearing them every day. Have more than one pair of shoes in rotation for everyday wear. Leather absorbs moisture from your sweat, and damp shoes are more prone to cracking and scuffing. Give shoes a day in between wears, allowing enough time for any dampness to dry out.

Don't step on the back of shoes

When I'm feeling lazy and just running out really quickly to get the mail or take out the trash, I'm tempted to just *slip* my shoes on, rather than put them on. So I end up stepping on the back of the shoe, with my foot only partially inside my shoe. You've probably done this too, but it's a terrible idea! This causes shoes to lose shape and develop wrinkling. Use shoehorns to prevent the back of your shoes from getting scrunched as you put them on.

TIP

Get a shoe bench or stool to sit on when you put on your shoes. You are more likely to take the time to put your shoes on properly if you have a comfortable place to do so.

Occasional maintenance of your leather shoes

While you should do some things every time you wear your leather shoes, there are others you only need to worry about every once in a while. And that's good news because some of them may be time consuming. You can certainly handle all these tasks yourself (and I tell you how), but many can be outsourced if doing them at home is too much for you.

Polishing and conditioning

Although everyday maintenance and proper storage go a long way in maintaining your shoes, you occasionally need to polish and condition your leather ones. Conditioning restores leather's moisture, keeping it strong so that it lasts longer.

Don't have shoe polish or conditioner? Thankfully shoe care supplies are easy to find at any shoe repair shop, shoe store, or your local drugstore. If you're buying shoe care supplies for the first time and feel slightly overwhelmed, a shoe store or shoe repair store may be your best bet because they can explain to you how to use the products and what you need based on what shoes you have. They may tell you a trick or two. You can buy a shoe care kit or just the individual items you need. Shoe care items include the following:

>> **A shoe brush:** This is a soft-bristled brush designed to clean dirt and remove grime build-up on shoes without damaging the leather.

>> **A soft cloth:** Any soft cloth will do. This helps remove dust and dirt on shoes.

>> **Shoe polish:** This is a special wax for shoes that provides a protective layer from scuffs and scratches and also provides some shine. Shoe polish should match the color of your shoes; it comes in black, brown, and neutral for other colored shoes.

>> **Leather conditioner:** This is a lotion that keeps leather soft and pliable. Leather loses its natural oils over time and begins to dry out and then crack and crease. Conditioners contain oils that penetrate the leather, keeping it pliable so it won't crack.

>> **Waterproofing sprays or waxes/creams:** These are products that provide shoes extra protection from water (see the later section "Using Shoe Protectants").

WARNING

As you can imagine, not all shoe care products on the market are eco-friendly. Many are made from petroleum by-products that are not biodegradable or contain toxic chemical solvents. A sustainable fashion consumer may want to avoid these. Look for eco-friendly brands that use natural waxes and oils, such as Pure shoe polish.

REMEMBER

You may have to polish your shoes every four to six weeks, but if you wear them often and they are exposed to rain and dust, you need to polish them more often, perhaps every two weeks.

You should condition your leather with a leather conditioner a couple of times a year to restore its moisture and prevent cracking.

Conditioning leather also protects it from stains. Some experts suggest that you condition new leather shoes because after months in a cardboard box, they may have lost some moisture.

TIP

Conditioning your shoes may sound complex, but it's actually pretty simple. There are lots of YouTube tutorials that you can watch to give you more confidence in doing it. All you need to do is clean any dirt off your shoes with a shoe brush and then get your shoe conditioner and rub gently into your shoes with a soft cloth. Let the shoes dry and you're done!

TIP

If this all seems too much for you and you have access to a shoe shiner on your commute to work or close to home, they can do the shoe polishing for you. While it may be cheaper to do things yourself, supporting small business is good for your community — and in this case, for your shoes (and maybe your patience).

Repairing your shoes

Even with the best care, your shoes may require some repairs. If you are like me and walk a lot (that's the New York City way of life), you may need to repair your shoes sooner rather than later. Instead of throwing your shoes away, consider taking them to a *cobbler*. That's a talented tradesperson who mends shoes, not a dessert. (Though I'm not against getting a cobbler on the way to the cobbler.) Cobblers can replace shoe soles, fix heel tips, and give your shoes a good polish that restores their shine.

TIP

How do you find a cobbler? Search for one on Yelp or ask around. If you live in a walkable town or near a mall, you may just stroll past one.

If you'd rather go the DIY route, you can do simple shoe repairs at home using shoe goo (a shoe adhesive glue). It's used a lot of by skaters who experience a lot of wear and tear from skating. You can use shoe goo to fix small holes or fix the upper part of a shoe that has come apart from the sole.

Considering heel and toe taps and sole guards

If you have dress shoes and high-end shoes that have leather soles (soles that are made from leather, not rubber) you may want to consider additional protection from the elements by having rubber half soles or heel and toe taps attached to the soles of your shoes. Heel and toe taps are made of either plastic or metal and are applied to the tip of your soles and the outer edges of your heel, as an added layer of protection, as these areas wear out fastest. Rubber half-soles are attached to leather soles for additional protection because rubber handles elements such as water better than leather.

Sole guards protect the soles of shoes from scratches, chips, and wear and tear. People who have designer shoes like Louboutins may use these to protect the iconic red-bottom soles.

WARNING

Make sure you get these services done by reputable professionals. If not done properly, the added rubber can offset the balance of your shoes and cause your shoes to wear out quicker, as you may exert greater force on the heel.

Keeping Your Sneakers Clean

Sneakers are mainstream now; they've gone from sports shoes to everyday fashion. If you don't have to wear dress shoes for work, you probably live in your sneakers most of the time.

Sneakers are comfortable and require less care. That's why most of us buy them, but we need to give them a little love and care to keep them with us longer.

Most sneakers are washable, including in the washing machine at home! How long your sneakers last depends a lot on whether (and how often) you clean them; otherwise, you probably throw out dirty sneakers that still have some wear left in them.

REMEMBER

Cleaning your sneakers is probably one of the best things you can do to take care of them, not only to make them last longer but also just to make them attractive to wear. Wash them often before dirt and grime become too hard to clean. (Once a stain settles in, it's difficult to kick it out.)

The following sections explain how to machine-wash or hand-wash your sneakers.

Machine-washing your sneakers

Sneakers made of canvas and synthetic materials are washable in washing machines. You can't machine wash sneakers made of suede or leather. If your sneakers came with washing instructions, use those, but here are some general steps:

1. **Remove the laces and insoles.**
2. **Place sneakers in a delicate bag or pillowcase.**

   If there is excessive dirt, please be sure to wipe it off before the shoes go into the washing machine.

REMEMBER

   You can also use a Guppyfriend bag to trap sneaky microplastics if the shoes are made from synthetics. A Guppyfriend bag is a washing bag that your place your clothes and shoes into when you throw them into the washing machine. It prevents microplastics from seeping into the water. (See Chapter 10 for more on reducing microplastics from laundry.)

3. **Wash on a gentle cycle, using cold water and a mild detergent.**
4. **Shake out any excessive water and air-dry.**

Laces can also be washed in the machine in a delicates bag. To avoid shrinkage and to keep the plastic tips intact, don't put laces in the dryer.

Hand-washing sneakers

When in doubt about the safest way to wash your shoes (or any garment, really) use the hand-wash method. Hand-washing is much gentler because your sneakers are not spinning around and banging against the sides of the washing machine. And you can get to the spots that need a little more cleaning and give them a good scrub.

1. **Use a dry shoe brush to remove loose dirt.**

   You can also use an old toothbrush.

2. **Mix mild laundry detergent or liquid detergent in warm water in a bowl.**

   You can also use baking soda and water, especially for white sneakers.

CAN DIRTY WHITE SNEAKERS BE BROUGHT BACK TO LIFE?

White sneakers are versatile and trendy, but they also get dirty easily. Don't rush to throw away your banged-up, dirty sneakers! You're likely to be able to restore them with a little TLC (and soap, of course). You can find a wealth of information online. Look to YouTube, Pinterest, or even TikTok for simple tips and tricks. I have seen some success with household items like toothpaste! Before you throw out your white sneakers, it doesn't hurt to try.

3. **Scrub gently with a soft brush like a nail brush or toothbrush.**

   Make sure you wash all parts of your sneakers, including the sole and the upper outer part of the shoe.

4. **Rinse and then air-dry the shoes.**

Using Shoe Protectants

Our shoes take a beating as we go about our day. They get wet and spattered from passing vehicles, so they need a little protection in the form of waterproofing and stain protectors. These shoe protectors coat your shoes with an invisible shield that helps repel water and prevent stains.

Shoe fiends advise that you spray all your new shoes to give them initial protection.

Waterproofing your leather shoes provides the resistance they need from water that dries out leather and stains it. Waterproofing also keeps your feet dry as these products bead water off your shoes. Most of the shoe protectors you see will be sprays, but some come in the form of waxes and creams. You should waterproof your shoes every three months — more if you live in a wet climate.

WARNING

Sprays are easy to use, but you should pick sprays wisely as some contain toxic chemicals. Look for sprays that are PFC-free, solvent-free, aerosol-free, silicone-free, and biodegradable.

TECHNICAL STUFF

PFCs (polyfluorinated chemicals) are used in water repellants but they contain forever chemicals that are indestructible. Nontoxic sprays use water-based solvents and natural oils and waxes instead of chemical solvents and silicones. Aerosols contain VOCs (volatile organic compounds), gases that can cause irritation to the skin. Some VOCs are carcinogenic. They also come in pressurized cans that are difficult to recycle and may not be accepted by your local recycling program.

Shoe protection that comes in the form of waxes and creams is mostly for leather. You apply these creams to the leather directly with a soft cloth. Look for products that contain natural ingredients like beeswax, orange oil, carnauba wax, and coconut oil, instead of petroleum-based ingredients.

Storing Your Shoes Properly

If you are like me, you may be tempted to step out of your shoes and just leave them by the door. But storing your shoes properly ensures that they retain their shape and have fewer scratch marks and less scuffing. Here are some storage ideas:

>> **Use shoe trees.** A good practice is to use shoe trees (see Figure 12-1) to help your shoes retain their shape after each use. Cedar shoe trees are most popular because, in addition to helping shoes maintain their shape, they help absorb moisture and odor. Yes, yes, shoe trees are an additional expense, but they're worth every penny to maintain your quality shoes, and cedar shoe trees durable.

TIP

You can make a DIY shoe tree by using newspapers — or just keeping the stuffing papers that come with your shoes — and putting them into your shoes after each wear to help them retain their shape.

>> **Use the dust bags.** Quality new leather shoes often come with dust bags. If your shoes come with dust bags, be sure to keep them for travel to protect your shoes from damage as your luggage is moved around. Dust bags can also be used to protect shoes you don't wear often from dust. Keep your sensitive suedes and patent leathers in dust bags. I reiterate — please don't throw away dust bags; they are your friends if you want to properly care for your

quality shoes. If your shoes didn't come with dust bags, check at a local shoe store. Alternatively, a quick Google search will reveal lots of online shopping options.

>> **Store your shoes next to each other.** Don't pile shoes on top of each other, as they will scuff more easily. Use a proper shoe rack, especially for leather shoes.

>> **Keep your shoes in the boxes they came in from the store.** This helps to keep them clean and prevents them from being squished.

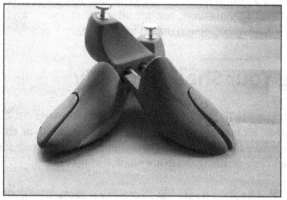

© Adobe Stock

FIGURE 12-1: Cedar shoe trees help your shoes keep their shape, stay dry, and smell less noxious.

5

The Part of Tens

Check out ten sustainable brands to get you started on your journey.

Shop sustainably on a budget.

Draft your shopping list for the thrift store.

Find sustainable brands for the whole family.

Get your feet in some sustainable shoes.

Chapter **13**

Ten Sustainable Brands for Every Budget and Style

S ustainable brands tend to be associated with a dominant style aesthetic of neutrals and linens, which can be a limiting factor if you have a preference for more colorful clothes and want to buy them from sustainable brands. I like neutrals and linens because they have the advantage of being able to be styled and matched, but I also like color. Many sustainable brands, especially recently, are providing more prints and more style options.

Sustainable brands also tend to be considered expensive, but there are affordable sustainable brands offering quality garments and great value for your money.

In this chapter I share ten sustainable brands, a mix of affordable, high-end, and size-inclusive brands to get you started on your sustainable fashion adventure.

TIP

Use this list to discover brands. You can find more on Pinterest, which has lots of posts with information, and resources such as the Good on You app, which is an online directory for ethical brands.

Loud Bodies

Fashion has a size inclusivity problem, and while the fashion industry has done a better job lately around fashion inclusivity, there is still work to be done. Loud Bodies is a size-inclusive, sustainable brand for women, with sizes ranging from XXS to 10XL.

Loud Bodies believes that fashionable clothes should be accessible in all sizes. The founder of Loud Bodies was dissatisfied with the dearth of fashionable clothes in plus sizes; clothes were either too plain or baggy, so she created this brand to address a need.

Loud Bodies has a wide variety of styles from romantic, whimsical dresses to simpler designs. Loud Bodies uses certified sustainable fabrics like organic cotton and new fabrics like lyocell. Loud Bodies also has an affordable line with many clothes priced under $100.

Wayre

Wayre is a travel lifestyle apparel brand. All its clothes are made from recycled plastic waste in a fair trade–certified factory in Taiwan. The brand specializes in travel *capsules* selections of interchangeable clothes that can be mixed and matched to create multiple outfits, so its clothes can be worn interchangeably, allowing you to travel light.

Its clothes are well-tailored and stylish, and you'd never guess they were made from plastic bottles by the way they wear and look. They use a silk-like fabric that is made from reclaimed post-consumer plastic waste. The clothes don't wrinkle easily and dry fast when you wash them, making them super useful when you are traveling. I have a few Wayre pieces, and they have been great on my trips. Sizes range from XXS to XXXL, and the clothes come in a variety of colors and prints.

Passion Lilie

Passion Lilie is a great option if you like prints and colorful clothes. Passion Lilie is an affordable, sustainable brand that is known for its bold prints. For my sustainable fashion blog, I have gotten to know some small brands quite well, and Passion Lilie is part of my sustainable fashion community.

Passion Lilie is based in the United States but makes all its clothes in India. It works with partners that pay good wages to workers and have been vetted for safety and employee well-being.

Its ikat-woven pieces and hand-block prints are handmade. Both types of prints are made by local artisans using traditional techniques. *Hand-block* prints are made using hand-carved wood blocks that are stamped by hand on the fabric. *Ikat* is a unique, complex dyeing process in which the yarn is bunched up and dyed in a specific pattern, then woven into fabric. You can only see the pattern after weaving the fabric.

Whimsy + Row

Whimsy + Row makes elegant contemporary styles. Its garments are handcrafted in small batches in its design studio in Los Angeles, California. All materials used for its clothes are either locally sourced, upcycled, or made from organic fabrics like organic cotton and linen. Whimsy + Row is size inclusive, with sizes ranging from XS to 3XL.

Whimsy + Row describes itself as a brand that eases elegance for a modern woman, and from my experience with the brand, it does! Its pieces are sustainable yet popular and timeless, pieces like wrap dresses, slip dresses, and summer linens in solid colors or prints. You can be stylish without compromising your sustainability values.

TIP It also has a resale platform where you can sell and buy preloved Whimsey + Row pieces at lower, preloved prices.

Amour Vert

Amour Vert is a great option for classic elegant sustainable basics. It's an American brand that is inspired by French style. Look to this brand for a flattering and comfortable styles in almost all clothing categories, including dresses, pants, tees, and even sustainable denim.

Amour Vert clothes are made from sustainable fabrics including a vegan silk-like fabric called Cottonseed Cupro, which is made from repurposed cotton plant seed fiber.

This brand also has a preloved marketplace where you can buy lightly worn Amour Vert pieces for less.

Mara Hoffman

Look to Mara Hoffman for high-end, luxurious, sustainable womenswear. It's known for vibrant, colorful pieces that the brand describes as celebrating women. If you think sustainable fashion is boring, you probably haven't seen Mara Hoffman designs. Even megastar Beyoncé has been spotted in one of its dresses!

With regard to sustainability, the brand uses recycled and organic fabrics and does not use any animal-based products. It works with ethical factories that pay a living wage and does site visits.

Mara Hoffman also has a resale platform where you can sell your preloved Mara Hoffman pieces and also buy its pieces at cheaper, preloved prices. Don't worry about getting clothes that are loved too hard; Mara Hoffman clothes really hold up well over the years. I have a Mara Hoffman piece that I bought preloved on Poshmark. After I had it for a year, it was still in good condition, so I was able to resell it.

Kotn

Kotn, just as its name sounds, is a great option for organic cotton clothes. Kotn is a Canadian sustainable brand that uses cotton and other natural fibers mostly from Egypt. Kotn only makes clothes from materials that are biodegradable and nontoxic, including the dyes it uses. Kotn has timeless designs that are still contemporary. The brand sells all the basics you need for your wardrobe, from jeans to underwear.

I love its essential crew cotton T-shirt; it's super soft. But Kotn has much more. In addition to more casual wardrobe staples like tees and sweatshirts, Kotn has comfortable workwear designed to be worn both in and outside of the office, including some suits. And all its clothing is available in inclusive sizing, ranging from XXS to 3XL, at affordable prices.

Outerknown

Outerknown is known for its jeans but also has classic casual staples like T-shirts, plaid coats and shirts, sweaters, sweatpants, and more. Outerknown's sustainable SEA (Social Economic Accountability) jeans are made under strict environmental guidelines by its supplier, Saitex, a leader in sustainable denim. Its jeans have high reviews for quality and environmental standards, and they come with a lifetime guarantee of repair and/or replacement. Outerknown also has sustainable corduroys.

Outerknown's style is understated but includes quality pieces that you can easily incorporate into your wardrobe. Outerknown's functional pieces include layering pieces like its best-selling blanket (flannel) shirt, knitwear, and lightweight jackets.

TIP

Outerknown also has a preloved section on its website, which is a great way to get pieces at a lower price.

Parade

Parade is mostly known as a sustainable bra and underwear brand and is also known for its bra recycling program. Parade is an inclusive brand with sizing from XXS to 3XL and features diverse models.

Sustainable basics tend to be skewed toward neutrals, but Parade has options for those of you who may want more colorful staples, such as colorful T-shirts, tanks, and crop tops. Offerings also include bodysuits, dresses, and loungewear.

Organic Basics

Organic Basics is one of the better-known sustainable brands for basics and wardrobe essentials. Just as its name suggests, its clothing is made from organic natural fibers, including denim made from organic cotton. In addition to cotton fabrics, it also uses recycled fibers like recycled wool.

Organic Basics favors simple, minimalist silhouettes that will easily match what you already have. It has a variety of T-shirts in different lengths and shapes that I haven't seen much of else-where, so it's worth checking out. Current sizing runs from XS to XL, but Organic Basics has plans to start offering inclusive sizing.

IN THIS CHAPTER

» **Working with the clothes you own**

» **Buying sustainably-made pieces at affordable prices**

» **Shopping for preloved pieces**

» **Renting and swapping clothes**

Chapter **14**

Ten Ways to Shop Sustainably on a Budget

S hopping sustainably is more within your reach than you think. Despite a misconception to the contrary, there are plenty of ways to be a sustainable fashionista without breaking the bank. You just need to know where to look.

Sustainable fashion is all about approaching fashion in a less wasteful way, and in this chapter, I share some advice on how to do better for the earth all while staying within budget. Key ways to save include shopping at thrift stores (Chapters 7 and 8) and renting clothes. I tell you how to make the most of the clothes you already have (more tips in Chapter 2). And if you're creative, you can upcycle a few items to create new looks. (See Chapter 11 for beginner-friendly upcycling ideas.)

If you really need something brand new but still want a sustainable option, I've got you covered. This chapter is a collection of my budget-friendly sustainability hacks.

Shop Your Closet

The clothes you already own, including your old fast-fashion pieces, are the most sustainable clothes you have! After hearing about all the negative impacts of fast fashion, you may just want to throw away all your old clothes and replace them with new, sustainable pieces. This isn't necessary and would cost you a lot of money.

TECHNICAL STUFF

Throwing away your clothes would also end up being counter-productive to the sustainable movement because you'd be adding clothes to a landfill. Even if you were to donate those clothes (see Chapter 9), you'd be giving them an unnecessarily short first life.

Fall in love all over again with your old pieces; don't rush to give them all away. Some pieces are worth holding on to — plus, trends always come back. I love it when I find an old outfit that I'd forgotten about. Before you donate or give away your clothes, give them another look-through. Recently, I had a pile of old clothes that I planned to sell, but then I saw an outfit I loved at a mall and realized I could re-create it with a dress I had planned to get rid of.

Take inspiration from the fashion you see in stores but don't buy. The overconsumption crisis is fueled in part by impulse buys, which frankly are primarily caused by the barrage of advertisements. Resisting can be hard at first, but it gets easier; trust me. With some willpower and practice, you'll be able visit a mall or other fashion hub like SoHo, New York City, and leave with lots of inspiration but no shopping bags. A lot of the stuff on display may just be a rearrangement of what you already have in your closet. You can probably re-create many of those looks at home.

TIP

To shop your closet easily, keep it organized! You'll appreciate what you own more when you can see it more readily. I like to organize my closet first by season, then by type, and then by color. If I'm looking for a tank top to wear with a skirt, I know to go to my spring/summer section, then look for tops, and then find a color that matches the skirt. Easy-peasy!

REMEMBER

While fast fashion isn't great, you need to treat your old fast fashion as you would your treasured pieces so you can keep them longer and keep shopping your closet. A lot of resources were extracted to make your clothes, including synthetic fibers that won't decompose in landfills. So make them last and put those fast-fashion pieces to work!

Shop Secondhand

Shopping secondhand, or thrifting, is a great way to shop sustainably. Thrifting is also a lot more affordable than buying brand-new clothes (30 to 50 percent cheaper), keeps clothes out of landfills and in circulation much longer. Most of what you need is probably available secondhand because so much stuff has already been made. If you're new to thrifting, check out Chapter 7. If you've been thrifting before but are looking to walk out of the store with winners more often, flip to Chapter 8.

Shop Intentionally

Shopping intentionally means buying clothes that you are going to wear and that will last. However, you may be accustomed to buying a lot of clothes often. That's because many of us live in a culture of excess, where people buy more than they need and almost anything can be considered disposal, and fashion companies profit from this. The mainstream fashion industry has created so much excess that you can pretty much shop all the time, buying a lot of stuff you don't really need. Shopping intentionally is a strategy that helps you shop sustainably and saves you a lot of money.

REMEMBER

Even if you only buy clothes from sustainable brands, buying in excess makes your purchases unsustainable.

There are many ways you can shop intentionally, even from brands that aren't considered sustainable. If you do shop from unsustainable or fast-fashion brands, find the best-quality pieces available and pieces that you can wear for a long time, not the super trendy items. A good rule to follow is to only buy a garment if you know you will wear it at least 30 times. (For more on the 30-wear challenge, check out Chapter 6.)

One method for shopping intentionally is to create capsule wardrobes. A capsule wardrobe is a selection of interchangeable clothes that can be mixed and matched to create multiple outfits. (See

Chapter 6 for details.) I like capsules because they entail shopping with the mindset of creating multiple looks from a few pieces.

Look for Affordable Sustainable Brands

A lot of affordable sustainable brands are out there. Yes, "affordable" is a relative term, but not all sustainable brands are selling $300 dresses. There are sustainable brands that produce quality sustainable and ethical pieces at more affordable prices.

At the more affordable sustainable brands, you can find quality organic cotton staples like T-shirts and shorts in a comfortable price range, and the items offer good value for your money. In Chapter 13, I share some examples of sustainable brands for you to consider. This list is not extensive, but you can identify other sustainable brands using the guidelines in Chapter 5. Find a sustainable brand that you love and that fits your budget, and then marry it.

Check the Sale and Preloved Page

Sustainable brands offer discounts and sales from time to time, typically around holidays or at the end of year. During sales, you can get sustainable pieces at 20-50 percent off, which means apparel that is usually over-budget may be affordable (for a limited time). Sustainable brands don't have sales as frequently as fast-fashion brands, but be patient. Those sales are worth the wait! You will be rewarded with quality for less.

Another way to get sustainable pieces directly from the brand at discounted prices is to check the preloved/pre-owned page on their website. Some sustainable brands, such as Patagonia and Mara Hoffman, sell lightly-worn preloved pieces on behalf of their customers. These clothes can be up to 50 percent cheaper.

Attend Clothing Swaps

At some point, you'll need a wardrobe refresh, but this doesn't have to mean buying new stuff from retail stores or even thrift stores. You can swap your clothes with other people. Your parents may have swapped your clothes with friends and family as a child, so why not partake in this fun, budget-friendly, and sustainable practice as an adult?

Finding a swapping community may seem challenging, but there are vibrant local swapping communities on social media, including Instagram and Facebook.

If you don't have one in your community, you can create one — you'd be surprised how many people are willing to join. Kids' clothing swaps are common in many communities; I believe many adults would also be open to the idea.

Check Resale Sites

On resale sites, you can score great deals on clothes from sustainable brands that may otherwise be out of your budget's reach. Sites like Poshmark or thredUP make it possible to get clothes from the more expensive sustainable brands, like Mara Hoffman, Stella McCartney, and Christy Dawn, for a lot less money. The apparel on Poshmark tends to be in good condition, so prices are higher than at your local thrift store but still lower than retail. Also, Poshmark allows price negotiations.

The clothes you find on resale sites are preloved, but that doesn't mean that they aren't great quality. Some sites even have filters that allow you to search for items in varying conditions, including "new with tags." Resale sites enable you to get quality pieces at discounted prices. Who wouldn't want that?

Consider Clothing Rentals

If you can't fight the itch to shop, maybe you can try clothing rentals. You can get the shopping fix without having to own these clothes. Clothing rentals are best suited for special occasion clothes, such as dresses for weddings that you won't wear much. One of the most popular clothing rental companies is Rent the Runway, but there are other companies like Nuuly, Armoire, Stitch Fix, and Gwynnie Bee. All these companies work similarly: You rent clothes for a specified period of time and then return them at the end of this period. The rental companies take care of the cleaning and will also provide you with prepaid shipping labels for your return.

There are also companies that enable peer-to-peer rentals. Brands like Tulerie and Rotate Your Closet are gaining traction. These peer-to-peer rental brands work differently from regular clothing rental companies where the company owns the clothes; with peer-to-peer you can rent right from someone else's closet.

WARNING While renting clothes is more sustainable than frequently shopping from fast-fashion brands, it still leaves a carbon footprint from shipping back and forth and cleaning the clothes, so use it judiciously.

Calculate the Cost per Wear

How many times do you wear a garment before you get rid of it or it starts collecting dust in the back of your closet? Many people only wear each item in their closet only a few times. They may feel like they've saved money because each individual item was inexpensive, but what they don't realize is that if they rarely wear that (seemingly) inexpensive item, the cost per wear of the item is actually higher than it should be.

Cost per wear (CPW) is the price of your clothes divided by the number of times you wear the clothes. You want the CPW to be low in order to have gotten your money's worth. CPW shifts your perspective on what is cheap and what is expensive; you realize that a quality sustainable outfit is cheaper in the long run than an outfit that has a cheaper price tag but is poor quality.

The price of things is more than the cost at the register; it's a question of how much value it gives you in the long run. For this reason, a sustainable fashion piece may not be as expensive as you think. And if you are shopping less, sustainable fashion may just be within your budget's reach. That timeless, high-quality, sustainable winter coat you've been eyeing might be worth the investment!

Upcycle Your Clothes for a New Look

Upcycling is another way to shop your closet (see the earlier section), but it requires some creativity and effort. Upcycling is creating something new out of something old or something you are bored with. It's a way to refresh your clothes sustainably from old clothes, or even non-fashion items, and making them into something new. Check out Chapter 11 for more on upcycling.

If you know how to sew, upcycling offers a lot of opportunities to create a unique sustainable wardrobe inexpensively. I've seen people make beautiful dresses from thrifted bed sheets and tablecloths.

There are some simple sewing upcycling projects you can do that will have a big impact. For example, you can change the buttons on a cardigan. Using some fun, unique buttons can really change the look of a boring old cardigan you've had for years.

Feeling left out because you can't sew? Well, a super-easy way to upcycle your clothes is to dye them — no sewing required! Look out for nontoxic dyes for your projects. Rit Dye has a big selection of colors and there are many videos on social media on how to use them. I've seen sneakers dyed fun colors. Alternatively, you can make natural homemade dyes. You can use avocado skins and pits to dye your clothes. (See Chapter 11 for step-by-step instructions.)

TIP

For more inspiration you can search on YouTube or Pinterest. Both sites have lots of tutorials on upcycling that will blow your mind.

Chapter **15**

Ten Perfect Clothing Items for Your Thrift List

While you can thrift almost all the clothes and shoes you need, some pieces provide better value for your money when you thrift instead of buying new. Luckily for you, thrift stores are flooded with donations all the time, which means there's a lot of good stuff to go around.

In this chapter, I focus on items that you don't have to buy new or at retail stores and that should be on your thrift list. Save your money from not buying retail while also saving clothes from ending up in landfills. Some of these items may even be much better quality than what is available in stores — especially fast-fashion stores, which tend to sell inexpensive, low-quality items. Take the items discussed in this chapter off your shopping list and move them to your thrift list!

Quality Coats

Thrift stores are flooded with all types of coats, and many of them are in excellent condition. What's great about thrifting coats is that you can try them on easily and, of course, the cost is lower.

Imagine finding a super-warm winter coat for a fraction of the regular price. I have found a vintage Max Mara jacket in pristine condition for just $30. Typically, a Max Mara jacket would cost $800 and up. Such a steal! But even if vintage is not what you are looking for, you can find a lot of options for everyday outerwear.

If you are new to thrifting coats, you may be overwhelmed at first by the sheer volume of coats in the store, so you may find it helpful to plan ahead a little. Decide ahead of time the style you want, whether you are looking for a parka, down jacket, trench coat, or wool coat. Go early in the day. Coats are heavy items and can be hot to try on, plus it's easier when the store is less busy.

TIP

Be open to thrifting off-season; the coat section will be less busy in summer and spring. Spring-cleaning season sees a lot of donations that may include some coats.

You can also thrift online. thredUP has a really good selection of coats, and you can filter by fabric, brand, style, and lots more. (For more on thrifting online, check out Chapter 7.)

Special Occasion Clothes

Special occasion clothes are great items to thrift because they can be expensive and are typically worn only a handful of times. This means the ones you find while thrifting are likely to be lightly worn, and you get to scoop them up for an affordable price.

Many thrift stores carry wedding gowns, and I have seen many people get beautiful wedding dresses for way less than retail price. Thrifting a wedding dress is not for everyone, but if you don't mind wearing a preloved gown, you can find beautiful, unique or vintage gowns for a fraction of the cost at a thrift store.

You can also find plenty of cocktail dresses, tuxedos, and wedding guest dresses at thrift stores. A lot of special occasion dresses end up on resale sites like Poshmark, so don't forget to check the resale sites. Reformation is a sustainable brand that is popular for wedding guest and bridesmaids dresses. Love Shack Fancy is a popular brand for pretty dresses; you're likely to find a ton of options on the app that are cheaper than retail and in good condition.

REMEMBER

Resale sites aren't as inexpensive as thrifting, but they still offer great finds for a fraction of the retail price.

Once you're done wearing your special occasion outfit, you can put the items back up for sale on resale sites. There is no shame in keeping clothes in circulation and making a little cash. Poshmark allows you to *repash* or resell clothes you bought on the app. I have *reposhed* a dress from a designer sustainable brand, and it resold fast. It's a transparent process, not a sneaky way to try and profit from your purchase; you are promoting extending the life of the clothes and getting some money.

TECHNICAL STUFF

When reselling an item you bought on Poshmark, you must *repash* from the original listing so that the potential buyer knows.

Trendy Fashion

Trends are cyclical. When a trend fades, people donate their now out-of-style clothes. But trends always come back, and when they do, those donated clothes are waiting for you in thrift stores. Lately, '90s and Y2K fashion are making a resurgence and thrift stores have plenty of this stuff, so you really don't need to shop fast fashion for these items.

On social media I've seen many people create trendy looks or looks worn by celebrities from thrifted clothes. I am not a trends-shopper, but the trendy looks created from thrifted clothes look impressive — more so because they were created inexpensively. Browse physical stores and online for what is trending and make a list or take photos. Then see what the thrift stores have; you will probably find something. If a trendy outfit captures your interest, break down the outfit into critical parts (maybe it's flared pants, a slip dress, baggy jeans, neon elements, or a sheer dress) and then search for similar pieces at a thrift store.

Nice-to-Have Luxury Items

Some things are nice to have (but not must-haves), such that if an opportunity arose for you to get such an item at an affordable price, you would jump at it. These are things you should consider thrifting. Stuff like silk blouses, cashmere, and luxury resort wear can be thrifted. There is no better feeling than scoring something luxurious at a fraction of the price, at least for me. I know so because I have scooped many items, like the 100 percent cashmere coat I recently purchased, at much lower prices than retail. This can also extend to coveted brands or cult brands; just know that stuff from such brands will always pop up on eBay and other resale sites. People who buy these items look after them because they plan to resell them.

Boss Blazers

Blazers are probably one of the easiest things to find at a thrift store, even if you're a lazy thrift store shopper. If you are looking for an oversized blazer, look no further than a thrift store. I want to leave you with some tips for scoring a good blazer because for a newbie it can be overwhelming. Keep these pointers in your back pocket:

TIP

>> **Look for quality materials or trusted brands.** Keep an eye out for wool instead of polyester blazers. Wool is more durable. Just because you are thrifting and buying at a lower cost doesn't mean you shouldn't get something that can serve you for many years.

>> **Stick with neutral colors and classic styles.** While thrifting gives you the opportunity to experiment with colors, neutrals are the safest bet as they will match a lot of what you have.

>> **Be open to altering.** Sometimes a gem of a blazer may be worth altering. A good blazer will serve you for many years, and if the thrift price is low enough, altering it may be worthwhile. Some alterations can be simple, like changing buttons, so keep an open mind.

Cool Leather Jackets

If leather jackets are your thing, you should definitely check the thrift store first. Leather not only looks great when it's slightly worn but is also good for environmental and ethical reasons. It's better to buy used leather jackets than to buy new leather. Secondhand leather jackets are also much more affordable.

When hunting for a quality leather jacket in a thrift store check its condition and make sure it doesn't have lingering smells; leather jackets are not cleaned often and may have odors that are a struggle to get rid of.

Dull-looking leather jackets can be conditioned to bring back the shine.

TIP

Fabulous Scarves

Thrift scarves because lots of good ones are out there and they're super cheap. They also come in one size fits all, so you don't have to worry about the perfect scarf not fitting you. You can even score some vintage silk ones. They are typically displayed close to the front of the store, in bins, or in some creative way. They're fairly easy to sort through, and you will rarely be disappointed. Some can be as cheap as one dollar. Read the labels and you may be surprised by what you find!

Cozy Knitwear

I love to thrift vintage knitwear because the quality of older pieces is usually better than knitwear made today. I've found a vintage Christian Dior with a label on it, and I have some vintage Ralph Lauren. But even if vintage labels are not your thing and all you want is an affordable sweater to keep you warm, thrift stores have what you need at a fraction of the price for quality knits. A quality secondhand sweater has stood the test of time and could become a forever piece for you. Here are some tips for you to thrift that quality sweater:

TIP

>> **Check the fabric composition.** Look for 100 percent wool, cashmere, or cotton, which are desirable fabrics over, for example, mystery synthetic blends which can be itchy and not designed to last.

>> **Sniff out trouble.** Knitwear is not washed often, so it can hold on to odors. While washing your find could probably help, you never know, so avoid the smelly ones.

>> **Examine the fabric's weave.** Good-quality knits are woven from long fibers and have tight weaves.

>> **Know the good knit labels.** Be conscious of brands and characteristics. Norwegian wool sweaters will keep you warm for years, vintage Ralph Lauren will last you many years, and 100 percent merino wool will be super soft.

>> **Consider a fixer upper.** If you find a wool sweater that has pilling, that can be fixed easily with sweater pilling remover.

Clutch Bags

You don't need to use only one bag until it falls apart to be a sustainable shopper. If you love pocketbooks, purses, and totes but don't want to contribute to the fashion excess problem by buying something new, you'll love switching to preloved bags. Thrift stores have a lot of bags of all types, and consignment stores and resellers have a lot of designer secondhand bags available for sale. Secondhand handbags are big business, and there are a lot to go around. Special occasion bags and clutches are also best thrifted because they are so lightly worn and can be scooped up for a fraction of the price. (For tips on sorting through accessories like handbags, check out Chapter 7.)

Versatile and Statement Belts

Belts are one of the things that always seem a little pricier than one would like; belts are typically made from leather, and that's always expensive. The affordable ones from fast fashion don't last long and tend to peel because they're not real leather. Thankfully, thrift stores have a lot of good belts that are cheap, typically under $10 compared to $60 or more for a good belt. Belts are easy to try on without needing to go to the changing room. You can also find some designer belts for low prices.

Looking for a statement belt? Having a Y2K moment or just need some fun belts to jazz up your outfits? Thrifting is a way to build your statement belt collection at a low cost.

Your Favorite Pair of Jeans

Vintage denim is one of the most searched-for vintage items because denim of the past was much better quality. Jeans were made better with much more care and a lengthier process, and for this reason, have remained in circulation for decades. If you find a vintage pair of jeans or a denim jacket at a thrift store, you'll likely find something of higher quality than newly made denim.

Denim requires a lot of water to make, so from an environmental perspective, it's better to keep denim in circulation for as long as possible by, among other actions, thrifting.

Need another reason to thrift your denim? Denim can be pricey, with a good pair of jeans costing over $100. Lately, even $100 denim isn't lasting long. But just like everything else you thrift, a second-hand pair of jeans will be more affordable than something new.

Thrifting denim can be overwhelming, but here are some tips to help you:

>> **Have patience.** It's hard to find the right fit in jeans even at retail stores, and it requires patience. Apply the same patience to thrifting jeans.

>> **Consider alterations.** Getting an exact fit is difficult, but if you find a good thrifted pair at a low price, small alterations may be worthwhile.

>> **Know your labels.** Know some quality brands so you can recognize quality denim when you see it. For example, 7 for Mankind, Acne, and Citizens for Humanity have great quality jeans. Keep an eye out for those labels!

Chapter **16**

Ten Family-Friendly Sustainable Clothing Brands

Environmentally conscious parents like me at times struggle with shopping sustainably for their kids. Sustainable brands at face value seem more expensive. For adults, you can easily justify investing in clothes because you can wear them for a long time, but kids grow out of their clothes quickly. Thankfully, there are options that are comparable in price to traditional retail brands that you may currently be buying your kids' clothes from.

Sustainable brands address the concerns parents may have about the safety of their kids' clothes. As a parent, you don't want the clothes you are buying for your kids to be potentially harmful to their health. (For more on the harmful chemicals used in some mass market clothing, check out Chapter 3.) Eco-friendly kids' brands market nontoxic clothes made from organic natural fibers, and credible organizations certify the non-toxicity of their clothes. (For more on certifications, see Chapter 5.)

In this chapter, I share a list of ten family-friendly sustainable brands where you can get eco-friendly, toxic-free, and ethically made clothes for your entire family. Many of these brands get bonus points for also providing opportunities to trade in or recycle clothes or buy pre-owned items at a discount.

Pact

Pact is probably the most affordable brand on this list. It was the first sustainable brand I found when I searched for affordable sustainable brands. Pact has all the everyday fashion basics except denim, so it's a great place to shop sustainably for the whole family. It has affordable organic cotton onesies for babies and all categories of clothing except jackets for kids ages 2 to 12.

I have a dress from the brand, and it's a good-quality dress at an affordable price, plus the fabric is organic cotton. It can be dressed up or down; it's a timeless silhouette. Pact has clothes in multiple colors and prints, giving it a broader appeal. There is something for everyone at Pact.

For Days

For Days is a zero-waste, circular fashion brand. (This means zero waste in the production process and through the end of the life of a garment.) All its clothes are made from fully recyclable fabric, closing the fashion loop (taking into account the entire life cycle of a garment) by making new clothes from this recycled fabric.

For Days clothes are mostly made from organic and recycled cotton. It sells clothes for adults, babies, and kids, so it has the whole family covered. In terms of style, For Days has timeless staples that are minimalist but still contemporary. It's also a good option if you are looking for more colorful basics.

When your For Days clothes have reached their end of life and can longer be used, you can send them back to the company via its take-back recycling bag. The clothes will be recycled into new yarn and made into new clothes. This keeps unusable clothes out of landfills. Plus, you get a discount on your next purchase. For

Days recycles clothes from other brands, and you receive a discount for recycling those at For Days, too.

WARNING While it may be tempting to send all your clothes to For Days, don't send it usable clothes for recycling. If your old clothes can be worn by someone else, you can donate, sell, or swap them. Recycling should be a last resort. Throwing clothing in the trash shouldn't even be on your mind. (Chapter 9 has more information on what you can do to responsibly offload your clothes.)

Jackalo

Jackalo is a sustainable brand focused only on kids' clothes. Jackalo has organic cotton clothes for kids ages 4 to 14. They're designed for play and to last.

As a mom of two kids, I get frustrated by how quickly clothes get worn out. After a few wears and plays, the clothes already have holes at the knees. Jackalo designs clothes with active kids in mind, clothes that will last and can be handed down. Its pants are reinforced at the knees so they will survive through numerous tumbles and have many positive reviews for being durable and comfortable. If the pants rip within 6 months, Jackalo will repair them free of charge.

The clothes are also designed to last through a growth spurt. Pants are longer (you can hem them at first; then take the hem out as your child grows), and dresses have bigger armholes.

Jackalo also has a trade-up program: When your kid outgrows any of its clothes, you can send them back in exchange for a $15 discount on future purchases. Jackalo makes necessary repairs and resells them at lower prices in its preloved shop.

Conscious Step

Conscious Step is a sustainable kids' socks brand, but for some designs, it also makes matching pairs for the rest of the family. Socks are an example of easy items to make the switch to shopping from sustainable brands. Socks are a generic product for most people, so why not choose a brand that makes them ethically? Conscious Step makes fun, comfortable, organic cotton, fair-trade socks.

Your purchase also has another positive impact, as Conscious Step has partnered with organizations like Habitat for Humanity, Room to Read, Oxfam, and National Urban League, and some of the proceeds of your purchases go to support their programs. A neat thing is you can choose what cause you want to support — saving oceans, planting trees, education, civil rights and equality, space exploration, mental health, and more. A portion of the profits from your purchase will support Conscious Step's partner organization of your choice. Conscious Step's designs are themed to correspond with the partner organization's cause. Your kids will enjoy selecting a fun design, and you'll love supporting causes that are important to you.

Patagonia

Patagonia is a well-known sustainable, outdoor apparel brand that has something for the entire family. Patagonia uses recycled and organic fabrics for its garments and produces them ethically. Patagonia is a to-go for many looking for sustainable outerwear.

It also sells other types of clothes, like pants, tops, and swimwear. Patagonia's commitment to sustainability encompasses both quality and durability, key elements in a garment you hope to love for a long time. Its clothes come with a guarantee that if you are not satisfied with its products you can return to the store for repair, replacement, or a refund. The company will also repair your damaged pieces at a reasonable charge. The website also has tutorials on simple repairs you can do yourself.

To help you find a new home for clothes that you no longer wear or clothes your kids have outgrown, you can trade them in for a trade credit. Patagonia will repair and resell those clothes at a discounted price.

Tentree

Tentree is a great option for casual everyday fashion for the whole family. Tentree has a wide selection, including clothes for kids and eco-friendly outerwear.

It has a lot of outerwear, which provides a lot of options for eco-friendly layering pieces. It has rain jackets, flannel jackets, puffer jackets, down jackets, lighter-weight jackets, sweaters, and hoodies. Its jackets are made from recycled materials and are animal cruelty–free. Insulation is made from vegan sources; Tentree uses Primaloft — a synthetic, toxin-free, cruelty-free insulation that's made from recycled water bottles. Its wool jackets are made from recycled wool.

Loop Swim

Loop Swim is a zero-waste brand that makes sustainable swimwear for kids and adults, and it's a great place for one-stop shopping for eco-friendly bathing suits for the family.

TECHNICAL STUFF Most swimwear is made from virgin polyester, nylon, and spandex, which are essentially all plastic.

Loop Swim swimsuits are made using Repreve, which is a water-resistant fabric made from recycled plastic bottles. The brand offers a variety of designs; in fact, my picky elementary school-aged daughter selected three designs she liked.

Loop Swim uses plastic-free packaging and sends a free reusable waterproof pouch with your purchase, so you don't have to use plastic bags to store your wet suits after swimming. Because Loop Swim is a zero-waste brand, you can send back your old Loop bathing suits, and the company will recycle them.

Many Moons

Many Moons, a kids' sustainable apparel brand, describes itself as America's first circular retailer. The name — Many Moons — says it all. The company's business model promotes keeping clothes in circulation for as long as possible. You have three ways to shop at Many Moons: You can buy new; rent; or buy preloved. Many Moons sells its own collections but also partners with other sustainable kids' brands. All the clothes it sells are high quality and made from organic natural fibers that are free from toxic chemicals.

I am impressed by its model, because it makes sustainable fashion more accessible by providing cheaper options via renting or preloved purchasing. It also reduces waste and the burden of figuring out what to do with clothes your kids have outgrown because sometimes selling or consigning can be hectic. When you buy new, you receive a return credit of 20 percent of the value. I believe those who can do more should do more when it comes to sustainability. Buying new starts the loop that makes the clothes more accessible to those who want quality sustainable clothes at preloved prices. I like that you can rent, especially when you need clothes for specific events.

Firebird Kids

Firebird Kids is a great option for older kids; they have clothes for kids up to age 13. Their style is comparable to more classic styles at Crew Cuts (J. Crew for kids). Its clothes are all made from organic cotton and are designed to last and be passed on. All clothes are made ethically in the United States.

Firebird Kids, like most sustainable kids' brands, facilitates the selling of your preloved clothes to reduce fashion waste. All you need to do is list your child's Firebird clothes on its site, and you will receive credit toward future purchases.

Mightly

Mightly has all the kids' apparel you need for babies through preteens. The brand has underwear, socks, pajamas, dresses, pants, hoodies, leggings, and even some sustainable rain boots and matching pajama sets for the whole family. Mightly has colorful basics and even features designs from emerging artists.

Mightly will probably be appealing to many because its clothes are just as stylish as the clothes you see at mainstream clothing stores, but Mightly provides safer, organic, nontoxic options. Your child won't skip a style beat. The variety is just enough and not overwhelming.

Chapter **17**

Ten Sustainable Shoe Brands

Y ou're motivated to get yourself some sustainable kicks, but maybe you're not sure what makes shoes sustainable. Maybe you're wondering where and how you can find sustainable shoes.

The footwear industry heavily relies on plastics and leather. Plastics unquestionably cause adverse environmental impacts and so can leather, when produced unsustainably. (For more on the environmental impact of leather and other materials, read Chapter 5.)

TECHNICAL STUFF

The industrialized livestock industry is one of the worst polluters. Also, the most common tanning processes uses Chromium (III) sulphate, a chemical compound that is associated with negative effects on human health.

Thankfully, there are sustainable footwear brands that are making sustainable shoes from biodegradable organic natural fibers like organic cotton, responsibly sourced wool and leather, hemp, cork (yes, the same thing your wine bottle corks are made of), recycled fabrics such as recycled wool, and recycled plastic. Some brands are even working with new sustainable fabrics like apple leather and algae!

In this chapter, I share a list of ten sustainable shoe brands to help you find a shoe company that can shrink your carbon footprint (the total greenhouse gas emissions caused by your actions) and shop ethically. Some of the brands listed in this chapter may place higher than others on the sustainability index, but all of them seem to continue to innovate, evolve, and work to make improvements toward sustainability.

TIP

If this chapter leaves you looking for more options, check out Good on You (www.goodonyou.eco), an app and website that has an up-to-date directory reflecting deep research on sustainable brands.

Veja

Veja is a sustainable sneaker brand and a great eco-friendly alternative for stylish sneakers. Veja's sneakers look similar in style aesthetic and price to sneakers from mainstream brands except they're sustainably made. Its sneakers include classic white and some colorful options. Unlike popular sneaker brands that have complex, not easily traceable supply chains, Veja's supply chain is fully transparent. It uses Brazilian and Peruvian organic cotton, fair-trade rubber, and recycled materials. Veja has sneakers for all, including kids.

Veerah

Veerah is a PETA-approved vegan shoe brand. Veerah uses apple leather, recycled plastic, and algae. Yes, algae! It makes dressy boots, flats, stilettoes, and even bridal shoes from these materials. Its shoes are on the expensive side but are undeniably beautiful.

TECHNICAL STUFF

Innovative plant-based leathers are picking up, albeit rather slowly because many brands have not figured out how to work with these materials.

Veerah uses algae to make form cushions. *Algal blooms* (due to rapid overgrowth of algae) are harmful for marine life as excessive algae clog their gills and fins. Algae overgrowth sadly occurs more often these days due to global warming and rising CO_2 levels. Veerah works with organizations that remove excess algae. The algae are dried and ground into powder, which is then used to make form cushions. So when you buy shoes from Verrah, you are not only purchasing shoes, but you are also buying shoes that assist with algal bloom cleanup!

WARNING

Although these shoes are made from apple waste and algae, which are biodegradable, plant leathers still require binding agents for coating, and these binding agents are made from plastic, which is not biodegradable. Not perfect, but an example of one of the ways some brands in the industry are reducing reliance on leather and providing alternatives for those who prefer vegan shoes (see more on plant leathers in Chapter 5).

Etiko

Etiko is an Australian footwear and apparel sustainable brand that makes sustainable shoes for adults and kids. It has a variety of sneaker styles (low and high tops), ballet flats, and flip-flops all priced under $100. It uses organic natural fibers like organic cotton, natural rubber, and organic dyes for its shoes. Etiko has a take-back program (Australia only), recycling shoes from its brand that can no longer be worn and giving a discount toward a future purchase.

Nisolo

Nisolo is a U.S.-based sustainable shoe brand that prioritizes transparency. Its leather shoes are made from Leather Working Group (LWG)–certified leather (this leather is free from chromium, a hazardous chemical used in tanning leather), and no effluent wastewater gets into the environment, and its sneakers are made from recycled materials. (For more on LWG, see Chapter 5.)

To provide full transparency to customers, all Nisolo shoes come with a sustainability facts label. Each label includes information on how the shoe scores against sustainability metrics like carbon footprint, manufacturing, health and safety of workers, and lots more. It looks like a food label! Nisolo has shoes for men and women, and also has a shoe recycling program.

Nisolo has a good variety of styles from boots to sandals, as well as popular shoes like mules, oxfords, and loafers, all beautifully designed and sold at a moderate price point (most shoes are priced under $200).

Wildling

Wildling shoes are interesting and different from conventional shoes. They are wider and have no heel. Wildling describes them as minimal shoes. Designed to be comfortable, the wide toe of the shoes is similar to the anatomical shape of our toes, and they are made of light materials that don't cause blisters. The shoes are made mostly from organic natural fibers like organic cotton, linen, hemp, wool, and cork, as well as some synthetic fibers. They're available for adults, kids, and toddlers. They are priced moderately, with most styles under $200.

They are stylish, modern, and versatile. You could totally wear them as you go about the city or take a hike in the woods.

Cariuma

Cariuma was founded by two board sports (including skateboarding) enthusiasts who wanted to bring high-performance, sustainable sneakers to the market. Cariuma is 65 percent vegan; it also has leather and suede shoes that it sources from farms that have high environmental standards and aren't involved in clearing forests. The shoes' insoles are made from cork and mamona oil, a plant-based oil that is an alternative to petroleum. Other fabrics they use are organic cotton, sugarcane, bamboo, sustainable rubber, and recycled synthetic materials.

Cariuma's shoes are affordable, with most priced under $100, and it plants two trees in a Brazilian rainforest for every sneaker purchased. And if you are a high-top sneaker person, Cariuma has you covered as it has both high tops and low tops. The brand also has skater-friendly shoes that are designed to last longer than typical skating shoes.

Ethletic

Ethletic is a PETA-approved vegan sneaker brand. It sells both high tops and low tops, and the prints are vibrant, with designs that are appealing to both adults and teens. Prices are moderate, with most sneakers costing under $150.

All Ethletic shoes are made from plant-based vegan materials like organic cotton and FSC-certified rubber. (Forest Stewardship Council [FSC] certified means that products come from responsibly managed forests.) The brand's rubber use involves no cleared forests, and workers' and community rights have been respected and upheld. On Ethletic's website, you also have the option to tip the worker who made your shoes.

TECHNICAL STUFF

Natural rubber is eco-friendly, but it's problematic if forests are cleared, workers are not treated fairly, and trees are destroyed.

Thesus

Thesus is a Canadian vegan footwear brand that is mostly known for outdoor hiking boots for women. Its hiking boots come in multiple colors and are made from natural vegan materials (natural rubber and recycled rubber) and recycled fibers (reclaimed ocean plastic and recycled plastic bottles). They're handmade in a family-owned factory in Portugal.

Thesus's hiking boots are designed to work in all seasons. They're versatile and can be used for hiking and for everyday fashion. The boots are moderately priced, with most styles priced under $200.

Good Guys

Good Guys is a French, vegan shoe brand. Its shoes are made without the use of any animal products and are PETA-approved. Good Guys uses a combination of plant-based leather and synthetic leather to make its shoes. It has a good variety of styles of shoes, from clogs to boots. If you like Doc Martens or similar mainstream brands, you'll love Good Guys' Chelsea boots, which are tough and stylish. Prices are moderate, with most shoes under $200 and a few priced slightly higher. All its shoes are made ethically in Italy, Spain, and Portugal.

Pozu

Pozu makes sneakers, boots, and slippers for men and women. Pozu uses organic cotton, linen, and cork for its shoes and is exploring the use of plant-based leathers like Cacti leather and Piñatex. It also uses recycled wool for its slippers and chromium-free leather. Pozu uses no harmful chemicals and nontoxic adhesives. Its shoes are moderately priced, with most under $200.

Index

About the Author

Paula Naggaga Mugabi is a New York City-based sustainable fashion blogger. Paula has graduate degrees in marketing and management and experience in banking and consulting, but has recently focused solely on fostering sustainability in fashion. Paula loves fashion and has spent a considerable amount of time learning the inner workings of every step in the fashion supply chain to ensure her work on sustainability in the fashion industry is properly anchored. She's also studied the science around the disproportionate contribution of the fashion industry to climate change. Paula blogs about a wide range of topics around sustainable fashion and sustainable living, including vintage and thrift, and fast and slow fashion. Paula blogs under @mspaulapresents on Instagram and YouTube, and you can check out her website at www.consciouslyinstyle.com.

Dedication

To my dad, the late Ambassador William George Naggaga. I know you are proud that one of your girls has followed in your footsteps and become a writer. How I wish you were here to read my book. I miss you every day.

Also dedicated to my dear mom, Mary Naggaga. Thank you, Mummy, for your encouragement as I wrote this book.

Thank you, Frank, my husband, for your unwavering support. To my kids, Kisa and Liya, for being my biggest cheerleaders.

Author's Acknowledgments

I greatly appreciate the support of the entire editorial staff at Wiley. Special thanks to Victoria Anllo for patiently guiding me through the *For Dummies* process. Thank you to Kristie Pyles, Jennifer Yee, Christine Pingleton, and Vicki Adang at Wiley for your support.

Thank you to Danielle Alvarado for your valuable suggestions in making this book a valuable resource on sustainable fashion.

Publisher's Acknowledgments

Acquisitions Editor: Jennifer Yee

Development Editor: Victoria Anllo

Copy Editor: Christine Pingleton

Technical Editor: Danielle Alvarado

Proofreader: Debbye Butler

Managing Editor: Kristie Pyles

Production Editor: Mohammed Zafar Ali

Cover Image: © Iuliia Bondar/ Getty Images